God Is Ahead of Us

Working on Our Behalf

by

Linda Handzel

What People Are Saying About Linda Handzel Ministries

"Linda is an encouraging and engaging speaker. Her messages and personal stories are both heartwarming and heart wrenching. God certainly has His hand upon her ministry. But don't read her book... unless you have a box of tissues at your side! Her writing is interesting, challenging, serious, and funny, but most importantly, it is God-honoring and God-exalting. Her experiences illustrate God's promise, "I will never leave you, nor forsake you." This book will be a great encouragement to anyone who experiences the trials and difficulties of life. In other words, every one of us. I highly recommend it." Pastor Dennis and Kathy Gonczy, Minnesota

"We have known Linda for over forty years and her cheerful spirit shines in all areas of her life. She has ministered in our church on multiple occasions and always leaves lives uplifted and encouraged. God has blessed her with writing abilities that convey Biblical truths in a relevant manner. Her personal journey of loss and sorrow has made her compassionate to those around her, and her gift of writing will be an inspiration and encouragement to all who read her books." Rev. Al Robbins, Jr. and Lauralee Robbins, Rhode Island

"We have known Linda for ten years; but you only need to be around her for ten minutes to know what is on her mind: Jesus is on her mind. She is a walking testimony of the great confession of John the Baptist, when he spoke of Christ, "He must increase, but I must decrease." Linda chronicles her journey through fierce trials with compelling and humorous writing. Her experiences will encourage you for your journey as you read "God Is Ahead of Us." Don and Linda Champeon, International Missionaries, "Training Others to Teach Others"

CONTENTS

Acknowledgements

God alone is able to make me stand, speak, and write. I cannot survive without Him and am grateful for His steadfast care. His love for me is greater than mountains and deeper than oceans, and I owe every moment of my life to Him!

I want to thank my mother, who is my biggest fan, confidante, and best friend. Her prayers carry me every day. Her stalwart faith has led me through life's many highs and lows, and I wouldn't be who I am today without her.

I also want to thank my fellow author, Doug Dial, for pushing me to write this book. I haven't seen him face-to-face since college, but through the wonders of Facebook he urged me to share my story with you. Sometimes, he gently nudged me, and at other times, he gave me a friendly shove. Doug was certain that my writings should be collected in book form, long before I was. His own poignant poetic writings are inspirationally driven and can be found at Authorhouse.com.

This book would still be collecting dust if my friend, Rebecca, had not agreed to help me edit it. And it would not be what it is today without the tireless help and constructive criticism from my faithful friend, Louise. Both of these ladies brought the words to life in an understandable way, and I am indebted to them in ways that can never be repaid.

Introduction

I have always wanted to be an encouragement to those I come in contact with; I want to pour courage into the hearts of people around me. But I never planned to write a book, least of all an autobiography. However, fascinating and amazing things have happened in my life that can only be explained as the hand of God moving on my behalf.

When Michael died, I didn't know how to do a lot of things. I did not know how to run the snow blower, order garage doors, or use power tools. Since then, I have learned all of that and a whole lot more. At first, if a problem arose that I did not know how to handle, it felt like I was taking a sharp corner in life's road, and I held my breath wondering how I would figure out what to do in that situation. But as I rounded that bend in my life, I discovered that God had already been there, and had taken care of the situation ahead of me. I learned not to worry about the next turn in the road because I know that God is already there, getting things ready for my arrival.

God Is Ahead of Us is a book of true stories that clearly shows His hand guiding me through life's many twists and turns. I pray that you will find help and hope as you read them, and that you will begin to see God's hand in your own life – always ahead of us

CHAPTER ONE

THE ACCIDENT

"Preserve me, O God, for in You I put my trust."
Psalm 16:1

Friday, May 25th, 2007 was unusually warm. I opened all the windows in the house and thought about how uncomfortably warm the church building would be for the patriotic program that night. Our ten-year-old son, Benjamin, had been practicing with the Christian school and would be standing in the front row singing songs of salute to our country.

My husband, Michael, had ridden his motorcycle to work and planned to meet us at the church building that evening. Usually, I would remember to bring a leather jacket and helmet for Ben to ride home with his Dad, but

I got busy with other preparations and forgot to put those things in the car. Ben would have to ride home with me that night.

The church program went well and was followed by a fellowship time where we enjoyed refreshments and visited with friends. Eventually, Michael told me he was leaving, so our three kids and I gathered our things together and followed him outside. The air was filled with the wonderful scent of springtime, and everyone was in a great mood. We stood outside laughing with the teens and enjoying the warm weather before Michael started home.

The kids and I left shortly thereafter, but stopped at a store to buy graduation cards on our way home. Sarah and Stephanie, ages twenty-two and twenty, were light-hearted as they helped me make my selections. Their eighteen-year-old brother, Mike Jr., was graduating the next day from a Christian college about four hours away in New Hampshire. We were planning to leave early in the morning to watch him graduate from that school's one-year program. We kept finding funny cards and were showing them to each other, giggling over the messages that were written inside. Finally, I realized that we had been standing there quite a while and it was getting late. We needed to choose cards and go home so that we could get ready for our trip the next morning.

Lights

It was dark by the time we headed home. When we were only three miles from home, we came up behind a long line of traffic stopped in the road. Up ahead we could barely see the red flashing lights of an emergency vehicle. When I realized we weren't moving, I called home to tell Michael that we were held up. He didn't answer and I thought that was strange. He wasn't the type to stop and visit friends on the way home. He was tired, and I knew that he wanted to get some sleep before tomorrow's trip. A few minutes later, I tried to reach him again but there was still no answer. I started to worry but didn't express my fears to the kids. The detour home was twenty or thirty miles out of our way, so we waited. I dialed Michael several more times, but he still didn't pick up. I didn't say anything to Sarah, Stephanie, or Benjamin about my growing sense of uneasiness, but fear was rising in my heart. What if Michael was involved in the accident up ahead?

A car pulled up on the shoulder of the road behind us, and a man got out to put on emergency outerwear. I went back and asked if he knew anything about the accident. He didn't look up but kept hurrying to get his gear on as he told me that he didn't have any information. As he reached into his truck to grab his helmet, I asked him if he would come back to get me if it was my husband's motorcycle. He slammed his door and asked what my husband's name was. I yelled "Handzel" while he ran away from me toward the accident scene.

I don't know how much time went by before an emergency worker started going to each car to tell people they had to turn around and go another way. When the man came to our car I asked if the accident involved a car or a motorcycle. He said it was a car and a motorcycle. My heart started racing at the thought of what might be at the front of the line.

I didn't express my fears to the others, but asked Sarah to park the car by the side of the road. I told my kids to wait there and started walking through the darkness toward the front of the line of traffic. My heart was pounding in my chest, dreading what I might find ahead. Nearing the red fire engine parked in the road with its lights flashing, I could see a big motorcycle on the ground. Lights from other vehicles lit up the area, but I still couldn't tell if it was Michael's bike because it was mangled beyond recognition.

A man stopped me before I could get to the bike and gently guided me to the other side of the fire truck, blocking my view of the accident. "My name is Linda," I said. "My husband, Michael, was driving a motorcycle tonight, and I just want to know if that's his bike." The man answered, "My name is Chris, and I'm a volunteer for the fire department. Someone will come talk to you in a minute." I didn't understand why he didn't say anything else. He just stood there quietly.

A few minutes went by, and a friend of our family, Craig, came toward me from the accident. Craig was the fire chief for the next town over. "Hi Craig," I said. "I just want to know if that's Michael's bike." Craig quietly answered, "Someone will come talk to you in a minute." I still didn't understand. "Craig, if it's not Michael's bike, just tell me, and I'll go back to the car." Again, he replied, "Someone will come talk to you in a minute." Then the two men stood there facing me in kindly silence.

My mind raced. Why wouldn't someone answer my question? But, I couldn't bring myself to say anything else. The fire truck was running beside us with lights flashing, people were moving around in the area, I could hear traffic in the distance, and we were standing in the middle of the road. But somehow, at that moment, none of it registered in my mind. I couldn't make sense of anything, and just stood there in questioning confusion. I kept looking at Chris, then Craig, then past them at the fire truck. Two different thoughts fought each other in my mind. The first was that Michael was in the accident, but he would be fine. The second was that it wasn't Michael's motorcycle, but for some reason the men wouldn't tell me.

Finally, a sheriff came and stood behind the other two men. He was a big man and looked easily over their shoulders to speak to me. "My name is Sheriff Cote, and your husband was involved in that accident tonight." I don't remember if he said anything else. I looked at Craig as panic rose up out of my chest and filled my throat. He opened his big, burly arms and I collapsed into them, sobbing. My mind couldn't accept that my husband had crashed his motorcycle. He was so careful! He had never had an accident in the 25 years that I had known him! I pulled away from Craig's embrace and tearfully begged, "Craig, tell me you made a mistake! Tell me it's not Michael!" He simply pulled me back into his arms, and for a moment he didn't answer. Then he told me that Michael's accident was serious.

I don't know how much time passed. Craig went back to the accident scene, but Chris put me into a paramedic truck and stood there in the open door beside me. I asked for a phone and called the church, asking someone to start the prayer chain. Then I called my friend, Rozina, and asked her to bring her two daughters, Laura and Brittney, to help me tell my children. Her girls had always been special friends and lived only a couple of miles up the road from the intersection where the accident happened.

I knew my children would be waiting for me back at the car, but I could not bring myself to go back to them alone, so I waited. Chris stood there silently beside me. "It doesn't matter how this turns out," I said. "I know God is in control, and He will take care of us." Chris nodded quietly.

Craig came back for a minute to tell me that the accident was "very serious." He said, "very, very serious" a couple of times, but I was sure that Michael would be fine. Still later, Craig came back to the truck again and told me that they were doing CPR on Michael. I knew Michael would be all right. They would bring him back. It happens all the time. At some point, an ambulance pulled away quietly and headed past the line of traffic toward the medical center, located thirty miles away.

After a time, Rozina arrived with her two daughters. We went back to the car with Craig and Chris. When we came into the glare of the headlights, Sarah jumped out of the car and ran toward me. She grabbed me and held on for dear life, sobbing desperately into my arms, "Mom, you were gone too long!" I didn't know what to say and could barely muster a reply. "Yes, I was gone too long." I looked over and saw that Craig had somehow wedged his husky form into the back of our car and was hugging both Ben and Stephanie at the same time. Everyone was sobbing.

We couldn't move the car out of the line of traffic, and I lost all track of time. We stood there between the car and the roadside ditch, waiting for permission to move the car through the accident area toward home. Craig kept wiping tears from his face, and I jokingly remarked that he was too tender for this kind of work. He just looked at me and shook his head. At some point, I called Mike Jr. to tell him about the accident, saying I did not have any details, except that it was very serious. I promised to call again as soon as I had more news.

After a while, Craig said he was going to let us drive through. Brittney drove our car, and Rozina followed in her car with Laura. The emergency workers planned to move the fire truck to block our view of the accident, but somehow communications broke down, and it did not happen. As we drove by slowly, we could see the accident scene lit up with emergency lights, and it was clear that Michael's motorcycle was under the front of a car. Everyone saw it, and Stephanie screamed, "There's Daddy's bike!" I'm sure the emergency workers could hear her wails through the open car windows.

As we pulled into our driveway, Mike Jr. called and told me, "Mom, if Dad is in the hospital, I don't want to stay for my graduation. I want to come home now." I calmly told him that he didn't need to come home until we knew how Dad was. It was getting late, and I didn't want him starting toward home at that time of night. But really, none of that mattered because I was still sure that Michael would be all right.

The Call

We hastily packed a few necessities, in case we ended up spending the night at the hospital. I closed the windows, walked the dog, and called my neighbor, who came over immediately. I knew the doctors would take care of Michael and reasoned that we would just sit in the waiting room all night anyway, so I wasn't worried about rushing. We lived forty minutes from the hospital, and I was trying to make sure everything was properly taken care of before we left. I did not realize that it was already 10:30 PM. Rozina was waiting for us by the front door, and finally she urged, "Linda, we have to go!"

I realized she was right, called the children, and turned toward the door. Just then the phone rang. Our cordless phones hadn't been working properly, so I ran upstairs to the study to answer the one dependable phone we had. My voice trembled as I answered, "Hello?" I did not recognize the voice on the other end that said, "Hello, is this Linda Handzel?" I affirmed that it was. "This is Dr. _____, and I work in the emergency room at the medical center." I sank into the desk chair and Rozina stood beside me while Ben listened behind her. The doctor continued, "When the paramedics arrived at your husband's accident tonight, he had no pulse, no blood pressure, and no respiration." Then he said something else, but my mind would not accept it. To this day I don't remember what it was. Instantly, I knew something was terribly wrong. My breath caught in my throat, and my heart started pounding in my chest, but the line was silent.

Finally, I caught my breath enough to force out the words, "Could you repeat that, please?" Around me the whole house was eerily quiet. Everyone was standing on or near the stairs, listening to my conversation. The doctor repeated the information about Michael's vital signs. Then he stopped and I waited, but he did not say anything more. I struggled to find my voice. My heart was pounding so hard that I could hear the blood pulsating through my head and even my ears were throbbing with the racing rhythm. My trembling hand struggled to hold the phone to my ear. Finally, I found my voice enough to quietly ask, "And could you repeat the other sentence?" There was a pause on the line, and it seemed that the doctor was struggling to speak. His voice was filled with regret as he said, "We were unable to revive him."

"In my distress I cried to the Lord, and He heard me." Psalm 120:1

I dropped the phone, put my head on the desk, and started sobbing. Ben lunged at me with such force that the wheeled desk chair rolled across the floor. He clutched me, his voice filled with desperation as he demanded, "Mom? What, Mom? What did he say?" I choked out the words, "Daddy's gone to Heaven." Rozina picked up the phone to talk to the doctor, but she had to keep asking him to repeat himself because Ben was crying in my arms so loudly that she couldn't hear what the doctor was saying.

Somehow, we all ended up outside and the sounds of crying could be heard across our lawn. Both Sarah and Stephanie were on their cell phones, sobbing as they choked out the news. Mike Jr. called back again before I could call him. When I told him the news his voice went into a soft scream mixed with a wail, "My Dad died?!"

Blessings Despite My Grief

I don't remember any more of my conversation with Mike Jr. that night. There are many things I don't remember about that evening, and the weeks that followed. I believe that is one way that God protected me. Even years later, it would be too overwhelming for me to remember every detail of that night. From that time on even until this day, I was, and still am, so amazed by God's tender, loving care of our family on that night. He knew what we needed and faithfully provided it!

I'm so thankful that we needed to stop for graduation cards that night. Had it not been for that stop, we might have been the first ones to arrive at the accident and seen Michael's body stretched out, face-down on the ground.

At the time of the accident, I did not know anyone on my small town's volunteer rescue squad, but our whole family knew Craig. He wasn't supposed to be working that night, but because of an unusually high number of accidents in the region he went in to provide cover, as all the responders from both my town, and the town he works for, were busy with other calls. He arrived at the station just as the call came in about Michael's accident, and the only vehicle left for him to take was the fire engine. He climbed out of his own truck and ran to the fire engine not knowing that he was responding to his friend's accident.

At the scene, the volunteer firefighter who had pulled up behind us found Craig kneeling on the ground and put his hand on Craig's back, asking, "Is that Mike Handzel's bike?" Craig was startled and said, "Yes, but how did you know?" The man replied, "His wife is back there in the line." That brief exchange alerted Craig to our presence there so he could help us.

After he left the accident, Craig went home and called several mutual friends of ours, waking them up to give them the news. Craig's wife, Corinne, was Michael's secretary at work. After making the phone calls, they came to the house together and stayed with us for several hours. Craig took Ben on a walk alone and encouraged him to ask questions about the accident. Craig wanted to assure Ben that his father's body wasn't broken into pieces because of the accident.

Along with the blessing of support given to us by Craig and his wife, we were aided by many others. Even though Rozina had a son getting married the next day, she and her daughters stayed late into the night until I urged them to go home. People arrived all night, including our pastor and his lovely wife, who asked if they could stay with us until Mike Jr. got home.

Mike Jr. was living with a family in New Hampshire and was planning to move home after his graduation the next day. When the father of the family, Phil, found out that Michael had died, he put Mike Jr. into his own car and drove four hours to get him home. They arrived around 2:30 AM, and when Mike came through the door our pastor held him in a bear hug while they both sobbed in unspeakable grief. In the meantime, Phil's wife, Kathy, and their two children, packed all of Mike's belongings into his car and drove it to our house. They arrived around 4:30 AM. Phil slept for a couple of hours in his car, but they declined my offer to nap at our house before they drove home. They stayed up all night for us.

Friends

I could write a thick book detailing the many more kindnesses that were bestowed on us in the days following that fateful night. I wanted to keep a journal, but my hands wouldn't stop shaking for weeks, and I couldn't write.

However, there is one couple that I will tell you about. Jim and Sandal are dear friends of ours from New Hampshire who always camped with us. They were among the people that Craig called that night. Sandal called me right away, and at the sound of her voice, I started crying uncontrollably. She kept talking, but I couldn't answer in more than one- or two-word sentences. I don't remember much about that phone call, but I will never forget these two words that she said. "We're coming." I found out later that they didn't go back to bed after they hung up, but instead took their motor home out of storage, contacted their employers, and set out on the four-hour trip to our house, arriving by 11:00 AM. While their motor home stood sentinel in our yard, they took care of us for eight days. They nursed us, chauffeured, delivered messages, cleaned, and did countless other tasks for us. They worked hard every day, never once asking for recognition or recompense. Later that summer, we found out that Jim had given up his vacation - a vacation they had taken every year for twenty-five years - for us.

"I will love You, O Lord, my strength. The Lord is my rock and my fortress and my deliverer; My God, my strength, in whom I will trust...my stronghold." Psalm 118:1-2

The purpose of this story is not to extract pity from anyone. Instead, it is to give praise to our wondrous God, who never fails. Within hours of Michael's death, I felt the presence of the Lord fill our home. As I walked from room to room, it was as if I was walking through a cloud filled with the Glory of God. I had never experienced anything like it before, nor have I since. His Presence was palpable to me. The intense awareness of His Presence stayed with me for over a week, reminding me that we were not alone.

I have never been angry with the man who killed my husband. The police report says that the driver of the car did not see my husband that night, even though driving conditions were perfect. Michael was going straight down the road and the man driving the car turned left into the motorcycle. His car broadsided Michael, throwing him through the air and killing him instantly. I know the police report calls it an accident, but Michael loved the Lord, and God has never had an accident. It was Michael's time to go Home, and that was how God chose to take him.

If Michael had not been killed on his bike, I know that he would have died some other way that night. I can wonder what might have happened if he had lived and how things would have been different, but it doesn't change anything. I know that God is in control of life and death, and it was Michael's time to go. It really is that simple, and I take great comfort in that reality.

That night as I walked up the road toward the red flashing lights, I was filled with dread as to what I might find at the front of the line. Then these words started going around and around in my head, "An open door... I set before you an open door..." That weekend, I found those words in Revelation 3:8. *"I know your works. See, I have set before you an open door, and no one can shut it; for you have a little strength, have kept My word, and have not denied My name."*

Since that fateful night I have realized that God's will for me was to walk through a different door, down a different path, and into a different life. I chose to accept that door and to go through it, and I have never regretted that decision. Honestly, this new journey has been bittersweet. I have needed God in ways I had never needed Him before, and He has met those needs. Although there have been barrels of tears, dark days, sleepless nights, and crushing heartaches, I still give thanks to God. I could never have come this far without His tender hands guiding, holding, and reassuring me. He is, indeed, a loving Father to the fatherless, and a caring husband to the widow.

CHAPTER TWO

I CALL HER MUM

"Many daughters have done well, but you excel them all." Proverbs 31:29

My mother was eighteen years old when I was born. By the time she turned twenty-one she had given birth to three children. At first, Mum spent most of our time together trying to stop the screaming...mine, not hers. Finally, after fifteen months, she desperately argued with the doctor and told him I was allergic to the formula they were giving me. He relented, and I stopped screaming.

I had a lot of food allergies that made it necessary for Mum to cook special recipes for me, but she never complained. Instead, she said I was her princess, or called me the baby-doll she had always wanted. Occasionally, I got sick because of this or that food I was allergic to. After I had emptied my stomach into the toilet, she would pull me up onto her lap and rock me. I still remember her lap covered with an apron and the soothing warmth of her care.

She tucked me in every night and prayed with me. I never questioned her love for me because it surrounded me daily. Sometimes she would look me in the eye and ask so seriously, "You do know I love you, don't you?" I was always surprised by that question because I would sooner question if the sun would be rising tomorrow than question her love for me. Years later I learned that although my grandmother had verbalized her love for my mother, somehow Mum didn't always believe her. Mum wanted to make sure I believed her when she expressed her love for me.

As a child, I didn't always recognize the extent Mum would go to demonstrate her love. A lovely example of this was the way she handled storms. Thunderstorms were a big deal when we were small. Mum would take us from window to window watching the storm, exclaiming about the beauty of the lightening and the wonder of wind and rain. When I was a teenager, I was surprised to discover that Mum was afraid of thunderstorms. She had watched the storms with us while ignoring her own fear, so we wouldn't grow up having that same fear.

Younger Than Most

Mum quit school to marry our Dad when she was fifteen years old, and sixty-two years later she is still married to him. When I was in school, all my teachers exclaimed to me how young my mother looked. She didn't look young to me – she just looked like Mum.

When my siblings and I were teenagers, Mum announced she was going to get her GED. It had never occurred to me that Mum didn't have a high school diploma. I still remember how proud I was when she passed all the tests. Cool, my Mum got her GED! I didn't question if she would be able to pass, because she had always been smart to me. She taught me so many things, such as cooking, cleaning, sewing, and ironing. Later, she taught me how to do most of the bookkeeping for the service station that Dad owned. Any mother could have taught me those things, but God handpicked her to be my teacher, and more importantly, my example.

Godly Example

Mum always made God a priority at home. Dad worked long, hard, dedicated hours building a family business, but Mum was almost always home. When we got off the school bus in the afternoons, Mum would stop everything she was doing and sit down at the table with us to listen while we told her everything that had happened at school that day. If a girl cried or a boy got in a fight, we told her about it. She listened intently, providing milk and cookies as we related our days' activities. When we were finished talking, she would get out the Bible and we read it together. Then we pulled out the kitchen chairs and knelt in front of them, taking turns praying out loud. When it was Mum's turn to pray, she made sure to pray for the girl or boy we had mentioned. This made a tremendous impression on me! Mum was listening when we talked, and she cared about what we said.

Sometimes I walked into the living room and found Mum kneeling beside the couch praying quietly and I heard her bring my name before the Throne of God. I was so important to Mum that she talked to God about me.

"The impression that a praying mother leaves upon her children is life-long." D.L. Moody

There has never been any question about Mum's faith in God. But never has it seemed more stalwart or resolute than during these last twenty years. Through times of trial and tragedy, Mum's faith has strengthened. She has been a brick wall of support in times of great storm.

My brother's wife, Lori, was diagnosed with breast cancer in 1998. Despite aggressive treatments and thousands of prayers, God took Lori home in 2001, leaving behind her husband, their ten-year-old son, and their six-year-old daughter. Mum was heartbroken to see her son suffer, yet amidst heartache and sorrow, she didn't question God. Instead, she prayed like a warrior for her family.

Three years later, there was a terrible hunting tragedy in our family. As a result, this same brother of mine who had lost his wife also lost his best friend and our cousin, Jimmy. This time shock and horror mingled with our tears and sorrow. Mum said God had a plan and there was a reason. Jimmy's burial plot was so close to Lori's grave that we had to circle Lori's grave in order to bury

Jimmy. The cold, misty weather wrapped us in gloom while tears of pain poured unchecked from our broken hearts and swollen eyes. It was unthinkable that we were standing by the open grave of a twenty-two-year-old man who had only been married for five months. Later in her kitchen, Mum remained as strong as a rock while I buried my head in her shoulder and sobbed uncontrollably over the tragic loss of our cousin. Mum's presence and her warm, caring hugs gave me immeasurable comfort that day.

Two years later, Dad had a catastrophic heart attack and was in a coma for five days. While Dad's life hung between heaven and earth Mum cried, but she never questioned. We quietly waited to see what God would do. Again, many people prayed, and Dad recovered.

My Encourager

Two years later, another one of Mum and Dad's three children lost a spouse. I was that child and I lost my husband without warning. Again, no questions were asked of God. By this time, the example of Mum's faith was planted deep in my heart. She has never questioned, and neither have I. Still, I don't know how I would have made it this far without Mum. That first summer, I called her every morning at 6:30. She knew I would be calling, and she always answered. We didn't plan it that way, it just happened. Every morning I cried, talked, reasoned, feared, and wondered aloud how I would ever run the house and emotionally support four broken-hearted children without my husband of twenty-four years. She listened, encouraged, advised, and loved me. Above all, I know she prayed. She told me all the time she was praying. To this day, she signs her e-mails, "Love & Prayers, Mum."

Two years after my husband was killed, my older brother, Floyd, was diagnosed with incurable cancer and was told he had less than five years to live. Our family prayed and believed for his healing here on earth. Floyd did very well for a while, but in October 2015, God quietly swept Floyd into His arms and took him home to Heaven.

Mum has watched each of her children go through unspeakable pain and loss in different ways, yet she has continued to trust in the Love of God. Her faith has been an amazing example to her children and her grandchildren.

"Train up a child in the way he should go, and when he is old he will not depart from it." Proverbs 22:6

Mum's influence is, indeed, eternal. A woman who quit high school and doesn't consider herself to be smart raised three children to serve and honor God. The power of her quiet prayers will only be clearly seen in eternity, but here on earth we see glimpses of their effects. Her first-born, Floyd, traveled on short-term missions' trips, helped the fatherless and widows, and served faithfully in his church. He took every opportunity to witness to his caregivers as long as he was able. I am her second-born and am serving God through speaking opportunities, writing, and teaching. Her third-born, Stan, is the pastor of a thriving Christian church. I don't think any of us ever questioned whether God could use us. Mum told us that God could use anyone willing to work for Him, and we believed her.

My Mum is a very smart woman. She knows where the true source of strength and courage is, and she goes there daily. George Washington once said, "All I am, I owe to my mother." I join him in that sentiment and know that I never could have made it this far without my mother!

CHAPTER THREE

THE POWER

"For Yours is the kingdom and the power and the glory forever." Matthew 6:13

On a cold December evening three decades ago, our Sunday evening service was filled with people testifying of God's power and goodness. One person after another stood to tell stories of God's amazing care and miracle-working power.

One woman gave thanks that she had to replace the driver's side door on her car. Earlier that year, her two-year-old nephew had climbed into her SUV while it was parked on a hill at the family's lakeside camp. Somehow, the boy had managed to get the gearshift out of park, and the vehicle started rolling silently downhill toward the water. However, since the driver's side door was still open, it caught on a tree and prevented the SUV from rolling into the water. That woman was giving thanks for the power of God that saved her nephew's life.

That night I was struck anew with God's greatness and silently uttered a simple prayer. "Lord, show me Your power." That was it – nothing more and nothing less.

"Since He has at His command all the power in the universe, the Lord God omnipotent can do anything as easily as anything else." A.W. Tozer

On Monday morning, I prepared to work on a Christmas tree skirt that was spread out on the tile floor in the center of my sewing room. Our baby girl, Sarah, was almost five months old and liked to be near me while I sewed. As I laid her on the floor, I realized my scissors were in the kitchen and went to get them. I was barely into the kitchen when a heavy crashing sound came from the sewing room. Sarah let out a terrified scream and started crying uncontrollably. With my heart racing, I ran back to the room, wondering what could have possibly made such a thunderous noise. Coming around the corner, I was horrified to see Sarah lying in a sea of broken glass. A thick, glass globe attached to the ceiling light had fallen to the floor, landing on the fabric beside Sarah and smashing into a thousand tiny pieces.

Tiptoeing through the glass toward her, I was hesitant to touch my screaming baby, afraid I might push a piece of glass into her skin. Despite her desperate wails, I didn't pick her up until I had checked her thoroughly, looking for blood soaking her clothes or oozing from her head and arms. Glass crunched under my shoes as I made my way out of the room, holding Sarah's trembling body away. As I changed her clothes, I marveled in disbelief that there were no shards of glass in them. How did that happen? Why wasn't she covered in blood and glass?

After Sarah was calm, I settled her into another room and went back to survey the damage. Broken glass covered everything in the room – the spare bed, the sewing table, the sewing on the floor – everything. There was glass in every corner of the room... except... from the spot where Sarah had been lying and extending out like a ray of light to the wall, the floor was perfectly clean. The globe had landed only a foot or so away from Sarah. She should have been covered in glass and cut badly by the broken shards. But instead, God had put His hand by her body so the shards could not hit her, and because they didn't fly in that direction, the area behind her was clean all the way to the wall.

"You are my hiding place; You shall preserve me from trouble;"
Psalm 32:7

I was also protected. The heavy globe could have landed on my head, neck, or back as I leaned over my sewing. Or, it could have broken beside me, cutting both of us badly. But none of that happened.

It took me hours to clean up the glass that day. It was everywhere, even under the sewing table and under the bed. For weeks, I found more glass every time I cleaned that room.

Why wasn't I on the floor sewing when that globe dropped? Why wasn't Sarah injured in any way, even though she was right near where the globe landed? God answered my simple prayer of the night before, "Lord, show me Your power." He had shown me His power in a life-saving way. We were protected by the power of Almighty God.

Sarah has since grown up to be a lovely woman, happily married to the love of her life, and they have given me a delightful grandson. My husband and I had three more children, and many more times God's unlimited power has protected our family. Oh, how I thank God for that power – the power that is His, and His alone.

CHAPTER FOUR

SHE WAS SICK

"Yea, though I walk through the valley of the shadow of death, I will fear no evil; for You are with me; Your rod and Your staff, they comfort me." Psalm 23:4

Her heart was racing so hard that the nurse couldn't count fast enough to get her pulse. Our four-year-old daughter mumbled incoherently while the medical personnel hurried to set up an IV. My husband, Michael, had left the day before to attend a work-related conference in another state, so I was on my own with our sick little girl. The nurses and I watched helplessly as her arms and legs broke into hives, and although she didn't open her eyes, she couldn't stop scratching. Stephanie was going from bad to worse right before our eyes.

It was Monday night, and she had been vomiting at home for more than twelve hours. Earlier that day, our pediatrician prescribed an oral anti-vomiting medicine, but Stephanie promptly vomited it back up. That evening, I put her beside me in our bed, where she murmured about playing ball with a friend who had visited her earlier that day. At 11 PM, when Stephanie's fever reached 104.9°F, I called the ER at a medical center thirty miles away, and the doctor told me to bring her in. I responded that every time Stephanie moved, she started vomiting, and I wasn't sure that she could make the trip. The doctor urged me to get her to the nearest hospital immediately. I picked Stephanie up out of my bed and started dressing her as slowly and gently as possible, hoping to avoid another episode of retching from an empty stomach.

Because Michael was away, I called a family who had expressed concern about Steph's condition to see if their teenage daughter, Michelle, could come stay with our other two children. When the father answered, I started crying at the sound of his voice. All I could say was, "This is Linda Handzel. Please, don't hang up!" The kindness in his voice assured me that he wouldn't. When I could get myself together, I explained that I was taking Steph to the hospital and asked if Michelle could come take care of our other two children. He assured me that she would be right there. I got things together and by the time I was ready to go, his sweet daughter had arrived.

I struggled to keep the speed of my car under control as I raced through the warm summer night toward the nearest hospital. Stephanie continued to mumble beside me. At the hospital, I scooped her out of the car and hurried through the ER doors where a nurse quickly escorted me into a room. I recognized the doctor as the extremely intelligent man who had once been our family's pediatrician and I was thrilled to see him. Dr. Beekman instantly remembered our family history of allergies and other medical information. God had gone ahead of us and provided me with the doctor that I trusted the most.

Dr. Beekman worked tirelessly through the night to bring Steph's fever down. He was optimistic, assuring me that the IV fluids and medications would help, and I would be able to take her home. But she did not stabilize, and by 5 AM, she was admitted. She needed to be taken upstairs to the pediatric ward, and the doctor offered to carry her. But she had fallen into an exhausted sleep, and I was afraid that she might be frightened if she woke up in a stranger's arms. Once again, I scooped her hot body into my arms and her long brown hair hung over my arm as I carried her out of the room in the ER. The doctor stood beside me holding the IV bag in his hand while we waited for the elevator to arrive at the pediatric floor.

I laid Stephanie in a junior-sized hospital bed, but she still looked pathetically small on the stark, white sheets. Dr. Beekman needed to get a certain drug through the IV, but he couldn't get the machine to pump as fast as he wanted it to. So, he stood there beside her holding the tube and the bag, hand-pumping the medicine into her vein. While he waited for the medicine bag to empty out, he urgently gave instructions to the nurses who hurried around, working on Steph's hot, limp body. Around 5:30 AM, as the sun was rising, Dr. Beekman left to go home and shower but was back at 8 AM, checking on Stephanie before he went to his office. At lunchtime, he came again to find that Stephanie's fever still had not broken. She was just resting quietly on the bed, much too quietly for an active four-year-old.

Stephanie seemed to be stable, so I called my mum, who came to sit with her while I ran home to check on my other two children and make phone calls. In the quiet of the car, I couldn't help but wonder if God would take our little brown-eyed girl home to be with Him.

My mind went back to when she was eight months old and had been sick for a week with uncontrollable diarrhea. This same Dr. Beekman had tried in vain to kill the aggressive bacteria wreaking havoc in Stephanie's intestines. The liquid antibiotics had only made the situation worse, and I was up with her several times through the night, changing her soiled diapers. Stephanie had never been one to cuddle, but instead preferred to use her swing or walker. However, when she became so sick that she could hardly move, she leaned against me as I rocked her by the hour, day after day. It seemed she thought I could make her better, if only she pushed against me a little more closely.

I took her back to the doctor's office ten miles away every day, where the scales reported that she was still losing weight. The doctor told me that he would have hospitalized her if he thought it would help. But he felt that Steph would do worse in an unfamiliar environment, so I took her back to see him daily instead.

Finally, Michael and I knelt beside our bed in complete desperation. Our eight-month-old baby slept in the next room while we sobbed helplessly in prayer. That night we opened our arms over the bed, symbolizing that we were giving Stephanie over to God in complete surrender. If He wanted to take her to Heaven, then He could have her. The next day Dr. Beekman suggested giving antibiotics daily by injection, saying he rarely prescribed such drastic treatment, but thought it was necessary. I quickly agreed, realizing this was a last-ditch effort to kill the bacteria that was charging through Steph's body. Within twenty-four hours she started feeling better, and within a week she was once again an active, happy baby.

As I drove home to get clean clothes, I tearfully recalled that evening three years earlier when Michael and I had desperately surrendered Stephanie's life to God. In prayer, I choked out the words, "Lord, I've never taken her back. If You want her, then she's still Yours."

As I returned to Steph's hospital room, Mum said, "A lady came looking for you. She wants to talk about insurance."

Insurance! I had totally forgotten about insurance. Steph's condition had been so urgent when I brought her in that no one had asked about insurance. My sleep-deprived brain raced through questions. What day is it? How long have we been here? When did we arrive? Fear filled my heart as I wondered if we had passed the twenty-four-hour notification deadline, making it so the insurance would not cover her stay.

I went down to the registrar's office to fill out the necessary paperwork, but I had not slept in thirty hours and my brain struggled to process the simple questions. She let me use the phone to call our current pediatrician, whom I had contacted the day before when Stephanie couldn't stop vomiting. His secretary kindly informed me that they had already notified the insurance company and that Stephanie's admission would be covered. Relief swept over my tired soul and it seemed I exhaled for the first time in hours. God had gone ahead of me!

"God is our refuge and strength, a very present help in trouble. Therefore, we will not fear,"
Psalm 46:1-2

Sitting back in the hospital room, my eyes burned like hot coals in my head. We were in a big, old, four-bed room, but Stephanie was the only patient in the room. I did not dare nap, though the nurse urged me to lie down in the next bed. I had been hospitalized when I was four years old, at a time when parents were not welcome to stay with their child. My mother was only allowed to see me for a few minutes each day, and I missed her unbearably. I have never forgotten that horrifying experience and have promised myself that I would never leave any of my children alone in the hospital.

Evening came and the fever was only slightly reduced. After his office hours the doctor came back to say he had been in touch with the Children's Hospital in Boston. They suggested a few things, so he was going to order more tests. But Steph would not be going home that night.

At my request, someone from church brought a hymnal, and over the next couple of days I sat beside my daughter's bed singing. I started at the front of the book and sang my way through to the back. Stephanie laid there quietly, listening to every word. I requested a rocking chair and hummed quietly for hours as I rocked her with the IV pole standing beside us.

Meanwhile, friends took turns caring for our other two children. God was taking care of us, rallying loved ones around our family. The church started a prayer chain for Stephanie, and people provided food for anyone working at my house to take care of the children. Michael kept calling to check on Stephanie, but every day I told him that the doctor thought she would go home 'today', so he stayed at the conference that his job required him to attend.

On Wednesday, the doctor said he had been talking to someone at the New England School of Medicine about Stephanie. He named a scary-sounding disease that he wanted to test her for. By then her fever was slowly going down, and she could eat a little. But her stomach would have none of it and quickly rejected every morsel. The new tests revealed nothing.

Friends brought Stephanie's six-year-old sister, Sarah, and two-year-old brother, Mike, to see her. They stared at their sister, asking questions about the IV, trying to understand why Daddy was gone, Mom wasn't coming home, and their normally active sister was lying so frightfully still. Finally, Sarah burst into tears with the enormity of it all. I had been so absorbed with the seriousness of Steph's illness that I hadn't realized how hard it was on our other two children. I felt helpless to do any more than I was already doing.

Finally, on Thursday, Stephanie's fever broke, and she held food down. Michael arrived home on Friday, having struggled for eighteen hours to get an early flight home. He helped me take her home from the hospital on Saturday morning.

"He's working on our behalf even when we can't see it all. He has a plan and purpose in whatever we walk through. He can cut a clear pathway through anything."
Debbie McDaniel

Although she fully recovered, we never found out why our little brown-eyed girl had been so violently ill. However, I will never forget the first follow-up visit for Stephanie to see Dr. Beekman again. He examined her, sat down to make some notes on her chart, then looked up at Michael and me with relief written all over his face and said, "We have had them come in that bad and not make it." I had known that she was very sick, but I did not understand until that moment that the doctor had been urgently working that first night to pull our daughter back from the clutches of death. For the second time in her short life, God had healed Stephanie from a life-threatening illness.

God is always walking ahead of us, preparing the way, even when we do not know what we will need. He is a loving Father, caring for us, and holding our hearts in His compassionate hands. I do not understand why God chooses to heal some here, and others in Heaven, but I do know that we'll find out in Glory.

Stephanie was given to us three times. Once at birth, the second time when she was critically ill as an eight-month-old baby, and again when she was sick unto death as a four-year-old. Eighteen years later, Stephanie got married and since then, she and her husband Andrew, have given me seven beautiful grandchildren. God is still ahead of us and He does all things well!

CHAPTER FIVE

A VERY PREGNANT CHRISTMAS

"For I know the thoughts that I think toward you, says the Lord, thoughts of peace and not of evil, to give you a future and a hope." Jeremiah 29:11

Three of our four children were born in summer months, so I was not very far along in those pregnancies at Christmas-time. However, I had been carrying our fourth child, Benjamin, for thirty-five weeks on Christmas Day. And while each of my first three pregnancies occurred when I was in my twenties, I was in my mid-thirties when carrying Ben.

My older age seemed to make a big difference in my comfort level as compared to my earlier pregnancies. I carried Ben for thirty-nine weeks and was sick for thirty-four of them! In addition to the nausea, Ben pushed against a nerve in my back that resulted in unexpected stabbing pains in the front of my hips. I recall walking along in a store when, without warning, nerve pain would cut into my hip, causing me to double over, moaning in pain. (If you're looking for an attention-getter, this one works.)

Our family had many Christmas traditions that were especially fun for the children, but that Christmas I couldn't participate in any of them. The children especially loved going to the mall at Christmas to see the beautiful decorations - tall toy soldiers, brightly wrapped gifts, and endless greenery lavished with gigantic bows. Every year the children were excited to see the beauty of it all, but that year I had to say no. Disappointment was written all over their faces, but they didn't argue.

Renovations

Our family was outgrowing our house, so we had hired contractors in September to lift one side of the roof and put in a dormer. Due to circumstances beyond their control, the contractors didn't start tearing the roof off that side of our house until the first week of December. Thankfully, the outside temperature never went below twenty degrees during the whole project!

In preparation for construction, we emptied everything out of the second floor and attic spaces of our house and relocated it to other places. We stuffed the camper with clothes, put the contents of the attic and the children's bureaus in the cellar, and dismantled their beds. There was barely room in the cellar for the children to open their bureaus to find necessary clothing.

I had always decorated the entire house for Christmas, but because I was sick and we were living in a construction zone, I limited decorating that year to putting up the Christmas tree. I told the children we would have to buy a pre-cut tree at the tree farm because my hips hurt too badly to walk through the field. They were disappointed because walking through the field to find the perfect tree was one of our favorite Christmas traditions. Michael was busy working all day and on the house every night and couldn't take them.

When the owner of the tree farm heard that I couldn't take the children out to choose a tree, she volunteered to take them out in the field herself. She patiently waited for them to agree on a tree, then helped them cut it down, and bring it to the car. The children came back with rosy cheeks, big smiles, and a great deal of satisfaction. They had found the perfect tree.

The girls slept on a pull-out couch in the living room and their brother slept on cushions on the floor beside them. I had been so disappointed to think we couldn't decorate the house, but they enjoyed falling asleep every night by the lights of the Christmas tree.

"Faith in God will elevate you to next level blessings." Germany Kent

I have no idea what possessed us to do it, but we decided to put a new floor in the kitchen and dining room while the construction upstairs was being done. We emptied the bottom kitchen cupboards, took them out and put everything in the cellar, leaving only a narrow walking path through the entire basement.

The flooring company had told us to have everything but the major appliances out of the room, so we moved our dining table and chairs into the living room and emptied the adjoining pantry and coat closet of their contents. The night before the flooring people were to come, my husband stayed up half the night ripping up the old linoleum. The next morning, I emptied the contents of the refrigerator into coolers so it could be moved when the installers arrived.

By the time the installers arrived, our house was in such a state of disarray we could barely move from room to room. However, there was still a small space in the living room, and my bedroom wasn't very crowded. I tried to figure out how I could keep the children entertained all day in those small spaces. Homeschooling was out of the question, but they didn't mind.

I thought the flooring men would move the appliances from one side of the work area to the other, but instead they moved the dishwasher, stove, and refrigerator into the one small space left in the living room. This left such a small path through the living room that I could barely fit me and my pregnant body through that space. As a result, I found myself in my bedroom with three energetic children, their eyes dancing with excitement as they waited to see what I would do.

I rarely called other people for help with my children, but that day I called Leah, a mother whose nine children had all grown up and moved away. I had never called her before, and don't know what impressed me to call her that day. When I explained the situation and asked if our children could come to her house, she was thrilled with the idea and offered to come get them.

I eagerly anticipated that a day without the children would give me time to rest, but that didn't happen. We had plumbers, carpenters, and flooring men all working at the same time, and they asked many detailed questions throughout the day. I even went to the hardware store for one of them.

The flooring job was only slated to last one day, so that afternoon the installers said they would carefully put the appliances back before they left, but that no one should be walking on the floor until tomorrow. Before I could panic about where the children would sleep that night, Leah called and asked if they could stay for supper. A few minutes later she called again, saying she had a short doctor appointment the next morning, and wanted to know if the children could sleep at her house, go to the city with her, and see the decorations at the Mall. She ended up spending the day with them, taking in the sights and treating them to lunch at a 'real restaurant,' something we didn't often do.

After talking to Leah, I called Michael and asked him to bring home sandwiches for supper—again, something we didn't often do. We ate together on the couch where we were at perfect eye level with the pantry and closet supplies piled high on the dining room table.

Through my fatigue that night, I marveled at how God had pulled everything together. The children were having a wonderful time with Leah, and the next day they would enjoy the festivities of the season that I couldn't show them.

"How precious also are Your thoughts to me, O God! How great is the sum of them! If I should count them, they would be more in number than the sand; When I am awake, I am still with You." Psalm 139:17-18

On Monday, January 19th, the carpenters completed their work on the upstairs, and on Tuesday, January 20th, the plumbers finished their work. That night, I went into labor, and the next day, on January 21st, Benjamin was born. I will never forget the amazing events that surrounded My Very Pregnant Christmas. God was ahead of me, taking wonderful care of our family, proving once again that He has perfect timing!

CHAPTER SIX

STEPHANIE'S PRAYER

"Pray without ceasing." 1 Thessalonians 5:17

We started homeschooling when our three children were ages five, three, and one. I enjoyed having the children home with me, but I was a busy stay-at-home mother, and three children were enough. Besides, every pregnancy had brought more sickness than the last one, and I did not want any more of that. So, Michael and I decided we weren't going to have any more children.

Every day, the kids and I started school by reading the Bible and praying together. I always asked the children if they had any prayer requests. When they were ages nine, seven, and five, somehow it became a contest to see who could raise their hand first to request a baby brother. During prayer time, they each asked God for a baby brother. Inwardly, I chuckled and shook my head. They were young. What did they know?

This routine continued for a year or more until our oldest, Sarah, decided that a baby brother would not be much fun, so she didn't want one. Our youngest, Mike Jr., realized that a baby brother would have to sleep in his bedroom, and he did not want that, so he also quit asking. Stephanie, however, never stopped asking. Over the next year, she always put in the prayer request for a baby brother. Sometimes her siblings would chastise her for it, saying, "Stephanie, would you stop asking? It's not going to happen!"

At times, Steph would try to nail me down, asking me why we could not have another baby. I was vague and non-committal in my response. When she approached her father about it, he was as evasive as I was.

Mrs. Foster

One summer while shopping, we happened to run into a homeschooling friend of ours. She glowingly reported that she was pregnant with her fifth child, and that was all Stephanie needed to prompt her. "Mom, you could get pregnant too, and then you and Mrs. Foster could be pregnant together!" She couldn't figure out why I didn't share her enthusiasm for the idea. Stephanie was only nine years old. What did she know? Somewhat impatiently, I retorted, "Stephanie, you grow up and get married, and then God will give you a baby boy." But she persisted, "No, Mom, I want a baby boy NOW! YOU give me a baby brother!"

We saw Mrs. Foster a few times during her pregnancy, and Stephanie whined often that she couldn't believe the Fosters were getting a baby, but we weren't. Her daily prayer requests for a baby brother vexed my soul, but nothing I said could make her stop.

On January 21st, Mrs. Foster delivered a healthy baby boy and named him Eli. We went to visit them, and Stephanie got to hold the newest Foster boy. It was love at first sight, and her eyes shone with wonder as she stared at the precious new baby.

Sure enough, we were hardly back in the car and hadn't pulled out of the Foster's driveway when Stephanie started in again. "Oh Mom, I have just GOT to have a baby!" Her voice escalated to a desperate, tearful wail, as she cried, "Please, Mom, can't you get pregnant, PLEEEASE!?" By now, Sarah and Mike were tired of her whining and impatiently snapped at her, "Steph, would you stop!? Mom is NOT going to have a baby!"

At home, Stephanie became more relentless than ever. She continued to pray every day in school for a baby, and then added the same request to her bedtime prayers. I was just plain annoyed. One day while I was working in the kitchen, she started begging for a baby again and I could not stand it anymore. "Stephanie!" I snapped. "God is NOT going to give us ANY MORE CHILDREN!" By the tone of my voice, she knew the matter was not up for discussion any more. She burst into tears and ran out of the room, completely brokenhearted. Despite her sadness, I was relieved that she didn't ask for a baby anymore.

"Then you will call upon Me and go and pray to Me, and I will listen to you." Jeremiah 29:12

A couple of months later, Michael and I left the children with their grandparents in Syracuse and went to a work-related convention that Michael had to attend in Tennessee. While we were there, I noticed I was unusually tired and emotional, but chalked it up to the extra energy that vacations require.

The day before we were to start the drive home with the children, I was in the bedroom feeling inexplicably sick to my stomach. Michael walked in and noticed that I looked pale. "Are you sick?" he whispered. "I'm trying hard not to be." His face took on a look of total shock and disbelief, as he asked, "You're pregnant, aren't you?" I gulped and responded, "I'm trying hard not to be!"

The day after we got home, I bought a pregnancy test, certain that the result would be negative. I had never used a pregnancy test before and stared at the mysterious strip with trepidation. Since the colored strip looked like a "maybe," I was sure it meant "no." I called the help line listed on the packaging and the nice lady on the other end said, "Oh Ma'am, if you see even a hint of color, you're pregnant." Still, I was sure she was wrong.

A few days later, I called my physician's office. By then, I had a lot of pregnancy symptoms, which I listed to the nurse. Her response was, "Well, with all those symptoms, we'll just make an appointment for a check-up when you're three months along." "OH NO!" I retorted. "I want a pregnancy test!"

A week later, when I arrived at the doctor's office, the symptoms had not gone away, but rather had increased in intensity. In utter disbelief, I realized that I *might* be pregnant. The doctor was chuckling when she walked into the examination room with the test results in her hand, and asked me, "So, what happened?" I stared at her, hoping I didn't understand correctly. "You mean, it's positive?"

I was sick for the next eight months. My nauseous stomach often revolted over a simple sip of water. Our children had to be quiet for hours at a time while I slept. When I took a nap during the day, they would cover me up and sing, "Go to sleep, go to sleep. Close your big, bloodshot eyes..." Later I would hear Sarah and Mike in the other room making noise, and then Stephanie would shush them, saying, "Shhhh, you have to be quiet! Mommy's baby is growing, and she needs her rest!"

Impatience

Stephanie talked about the baby incessantly. We grew weary of her constant, excited chatter. She found a book about prenatal development and devoured every word. Reports from Stephanie about our baby's growth stages were a common occurrence at the family supper table.

She wanted to see my belly all the time. She wasn't content to see the outline through my shirt because she wanted to see "the baby." I could not stand this 24/7 discussion of my rounding belly and the baby's growth. I was sick night and day and had very little patience for her endless banter.

As the baby grew, he pushed against nerves in my back, causing stabbing pains to shoot through my hips. The sudden stabs came and went without warning, causing me to double over, groaning in pain. That pain, combined with my overwhelming exhaustion and constant nausea left me with no patience for Steph's persistent chatter about the baby, so I told her that she could only discuss the baby with me once a week.

It was a Herculean effort for her to suppress her enthusiasm and she only lasted a couple of weeks. One day, I was sitting beside her on the couch going over her schoolwork and she was unusually frustrated with the lesson. When I questioned why she was so upset, she blurted out through hot, frustrated tears, "Mom, I just want to see what your belly looks like!" I realized that I had not begun to understand her complete love for our baby. With this new insight, I worked harder to be patient with her.

Stephanie repeatedly promised that she would help when the baby came, and started a running count to my due date, which was January 28th. At the seven-month mark, I had a sonogram and wasn't surprised to see that the baby's face looked just like my other three babies. I told the technician I didn't want to know the gender, but somehow, I knew. If God would give Stephanie the baby she so desperately desired, He would surely give her a boy.

Delivery

Waking up on January 21st, I knew. "This is the day." Michael woke the children, and a friend came to stay with them while we went to the hospital. After a long morning, the baby was born in the early afternoon. It was a natural childbirth, but a difficult one. I fought to get the head out, but then the shoulders were too broad to come together. The doctor struggled to get one shoulder, then the other out. She knew that Stephanie wanted a boy, and said, "This had better be a boy with a head and shoulders this big!" Sure enough, when he was finally delivered it was the boy Stephanie had prayed for. Baby Benjamin was born on January 21st, exactly one year to the day after baby Eli Foster.

> ## *"If you believe in a God who controls the big things, you have to believe in a God who controls the little things."*
> ## *Elisabeth Elliot*

Up until a few years ago, I told this story to illustrate that God hears even the youngest of prayers, and He has a wonderful sense of humor. But this story has taken on a different light since my husband, Michael, was killed instantly in an accident in May 2007.

At first, I thought Ben was Stephanie's baby. Soon after we told the children I was pregnant, Stephanie confessed that she had been praying harder than ever that I would have a baby. She did help tremendously with him, often sacrificing her own time to aid in his care.

Then I decided that Ben had been given for my husband. They absolutely adored each other and spent every available moment together. Benjamin called his father at work every day, asking questions like, "Who's playing football on TV tonight, Dad?" or "Want to go golfing tonight, Dad?" or "Can you come home early?"

But now, I see that Benjamin was given for me. When Michael was killed, our other three children were eighteen, twenty, and twenty-two years old. I could have fooled myself into believing that they could make it without me. But Ben was only ten years old, and his little heart was crushed into a thousand pieces. I had to hold myself together while he fell apart.

Countless times that first summer, I woke up dreading the day ahead, never wanting to get out of bed again. Then I remembered that a brokenhearted little boy would wake up in a few minutes knowing that Daddy wasn't there to give him a morning hug. Every day I forced myself to get out of bed so I could help that little boy find his way through dark halls of crushing grief. God gave Benjamin to me so I would have a reason to live.

God has a perfect plan every day, all the time. We don't understand it, but that doesn't diminish its perfection. God was going ahead of me by inspiring Stephanie to pray without wavering. Because of her prayers, Benjamin was born. He has his father's thick Polish bone build, wavy brown hair, and dancing brown eyes. In fact, Ben doesn't look anything like me. I'm so thankful to God that I have a son who reminds me of his father - a son who was given for me.

"Marvelous are Your works, and that my soul knows very well."
Psalm 139:14b

CHAPTER SEVEN

THE DECISION

*"You who fear the Lord, trust in the Lord; He is their help
and their shield." Psalm 115:11*

I attended a Christian school my last year of senior high, and that's when I met my future sister-in-law, Lori. I always thought she was beautifully composed, and in that regard, nothing like me. We spent a lot of time together, but my brother, Stan, spent more time with her than I did. After they graduated from high school, he went to an out-of-state college for a year and I was able to steal more time with her. When Stan came home at Christmas, he asked Lori to marry him, and the next summer I was a bridesmaid in their wedding. The weekend immediately following, she was the Matron of Honor in my wedding. Yes – my family had two weddings in seven days.

When my husband and I got married, we moved a few towns away from where I had grown up, but Lori and Stan stayed in the area. We had our first three children in seven years, and a few years after that, Stan and Lori gave birth to a boy, and then a girl. Our lives got busier and we saw each other at various family gatherings, but not as much as we would have liked.

When both couples had been married for sixteen years, our families got together for an Independence Day picnic. That day, Lori pulled me aside and quietly told me that she had found a lump in her breast and the doctor had ordered a biopsy. She said she was scared. Cancer was so rampant in her family that when she was only thirty-three years old, she had paid out-of-pocket for a baseline mammogram in case she needed it for future reference. Now, only four years later, she was telling me that she had found a lump. I knew there was no way a woman that young could have breast cancer. Her sister had a lot of problems with cysts, and I was sure that would be the diagnosis.

At home, I waited with bated breath for the biopsy report to come back. Mum's voice was quiet and low when she called a few days later to tell me the results. "The news isn't good. It's aggressive Carcinoma." I felt like someone had punched me, and my body spun around with the impact of those words. My whole world came to a crashing halt, and I could not think of anything else – my brother's beloved sweetheart, my dear friend had cancer.

Wrestling

For several weeks my mind rocked and whirled with countless reactions. I had trouble sleeping, and when I did finally sleep, I woke up thinking about Lori's cancer. How could this possibly happen? I couldn't fathom the magnitude of the implications that this diagnosis represented. My whole thought life revolved around Lori and Stan and her diagnosis. I lost my appetite and dropped fifteen pounds in a couple of months.

I knew what I would say to someone who came to me with this diagnosis in their family. I would say things like, "God works all things out for His good. He will give you the strength to go through this. He is still a healing God, and you can believe Him to heal her, here on earth, or in heaven with Him. Either way, He will give you the strength to make it through. God will take care of their two children." I found myself questioning every phrase.

Did I really believe this stuff? Memory verses from childhood had never been tested like this before, and my faith was shaken to the core. I questioned the very foundation of all that I had lived for since childhood. What if God isn't really all I said He was? Does He really care? Is He able to heal? If he did not heal Lori, would He carry us through this horrifying journey? Just the thought of my broken-hearted brother and their two young children (ages four and eight) was more than I could bear. Stan was a pastor; how could God even think of allowing Lori to have cancer?

Lori's treatment plan was laid out: a radical mastectomy followed by aggressive chemotherapy and radiation. Dozens of foreign-sounding medical terms were thrown around while each of us reeled with the reality of the unfathomable, and I questioned, "WHERE IS GOD?"

Mom and Dad struggled while watching their son's heartbreaking trial. Our whole family was cut to the core. I kept thinking of all the reasons this should not be happening to us. Mom and Dad had brought us up in a Christian home and each of us had received Christ as our Savior while still children. Then each of us had chosen a Christian spouse, and now we were raising our own children in Godly homes. Each of us was deeply involved in his or her own church. I mentally checked off all the things that we were doing right. Yet in spite of doing all the right things, it felt like everything was going wrong. I walked around in a dark cloud of despair knowing I was supposed to find solace in God, but wondering if I believed in that source anymore. I questioned every word of the Sunday sermons, wondering if the Bible was credible enough to carry us through this dark reality.

Maybe God did not care; He sure wasn't acting like He cared. Maybe I could not trust Him at all. Maybe I could find someone else to trust. Maybe I had been misled as a child, and God was not Who I thought He was. Maybe I should just give up on this whole thing called Christianity. It sure wasn't working out for the good that I wanted!

For three weeks I wallowed in my gut-wrenching doubts. I was so mired in anxious confusion that I didn't realize I was sighing all the time. I felt like the weight of the world was on my shoulders, and I was helpless to get out from under it. Nothing happened when I prayed, and all the words seemed hollow. What was I going to do? I was in the deepest spiritual valley of my life.

"With God, you are stronger than your struggles and more fierce than your fears. God provides comfort and strength to those who trust in Him. Be encouraged, keep standing and know that everything's going to be alright." Germany Kent

Finally, I started to recount the many ways that God had clearly answered prayers throughout my life.

> *On two separate occasions, my daughter, Stephanie, had been catastrophically ill, and God had fully restored her back to health. Who else could answer like that?*

> *I had always known that God was with me through every turn in my life. I felt His presence as a young mother taking care of energetic children. On countless occasions, He led me to make quick decisions for their care and well-being. Who else offered me that kind of companionship?*

I had seen God perform many miracles. One time, my husband unknowingly caught his shirt on fire in our camper and a man standing there was able to put it out before the fire got out of control.

I remembered car accidents that were narrowly averted on slippery roads, and other times when we barely missed hitting moose in the roadway. Who else was capable of protecting us like that?

I was hanging laundry outside one day when one question suddenly stood out above all the others. If I abandoned my belief in God, who could possibly take His place?

My racing thoughts came to a sudden standstill as I faced that one ultimate question: WHO ELSE IS THERE TO TRUST? Right there, standing under the clothes line, I concluded that there was NO ONE else that I could trust like God.

With that decision I felt a huge weight lift from my heart and took a deep breath for the first time in weeks. Relief washed through my soul as I resolved that I needed God and God alone. He was the only One who promised that He would never leave me or forsake me. I had never once felt abandoned by Him, and He was the only One who said, *"When you pass through the water, I will be with you; and through the rivers, they shall not overflow you. When you walk through the fire, you shall not be burned, nor shall the flame scorch you. For I am the Lord your God, the Holy One of Israel, your Savior." Isaiah 43:2-3*

YES, I was going to trust God and cling to His unchanging hand. I would believe that He would hold my family as we traveled this scary road. And from that day forward, I never questioned the foundation of my faith again.

"Therefore, I say to you, whatever things you ask when you pray, believe that you receive them, and you shall have them." Mark 11:24

The journey that our family took with Lori was not easy, as it was fraught with highs and lows. She finished her cancer treatments and felt better for a few months. But sixteen months after the first biopsy, she was diagnosed with bone cancer. In desperation, Stan took Lori to Mexico for alternative treatment, and we prayed. Oh, how we prayed! I'm sure that many thousands of prayers were offered, asking God to heal Lori. And He did heal her. At dawn on a quiet June morning in 2001, my phone rang with the news that Lori had gone to Heaven. I remember so well that it was a wonderfully clear day, a perfect day to fly to Heaven. Lori was only sick with cancer for twenty-three months, and then she was made perfectly whole.

When I decided God was the only answer for me, I had no way of knowing I was choosing a platform that would hold me through many tears and heartbreaks to come. I see now that God was preparing the way ahead of me, because the next fifteen years were filled with one heartbreak after another for our family. In my mind it seems that only old people should be in caskets, but I have seen too many young bodies there instead. We will understand it all when we meet Him and our loved ones in Glory. Until then, I am thankful for the decision I made twenty years ago to believe that God is in control and will carry us through every part of life. Because He is, and He has!

CHAPTER EIGHT

A CLOSED WINDOW AND AN OPEN DOOR

"In all your ways acknowledge Him, and He shall direct your paths." Proverbs 3:6

I couldn't bear the thought that I might never see her again. My precious friend was dying of cancer, and only the closest family members were welcome to visit her. I was beside myself with the sense of loss – loss in the present, and loss to come.

I tried to think of ways I could show up even though I wasn't welcome, but soon realized that behaving like that would only make things harder for my friend's family. With hot, disappointed tears, I resigned myself to the heartbreaking situation.

The next Sunday, our pastor announced that an elderly woman in the congregation was dying of cancer, and if we wanted to see her, we needed to visit soon. I took a deep breath and made an important decision. If I wasn't welcome to visit my friend, then I would go visit where I was welcome.

I called the elderly woman's family and took our children with me to visit at the appointed time. We were warmly welcomed by the dying woman and her niece, Carol, who was taking care of her. We sang a few songs, chatted, laughed a little, and went home. Carol called a couple of days later and thanked me profusely for the visit. I gained a slight solace for my soul to find that someone else was helped while I was hurting. We developed a wonderful friendship, and I helped Carol make funeral arrangements when her aunt died.

"You will show me the path of life;"
Psalm 16:11

Soon after that first visit, Carol and her husband, Dick, started attending our church. I believed that Carol was probably saved but didn't think Dick was. We visited them occasionally and were pleased that they continued to attend church.

A few months after Carol's aunt died, our pastor gave a moving sermon about fishing and wove it into the gospel message. I do believe God speaks to a Christian's heart if they are willing to hear, and on that day, as we stood for the last hymn, God spoke to my heart. "Go over and ask Dick if he wants to get saved today."

My heart was pounding as I waited for the pastor to finish his final prayer. As soon as he said, "Amen," I bolted for the pew where Carol and Dick were sitting. I knew if I waited, I might lose courage.

I sat down beside Dick, looked him straight in the eyes, and said, "Dick, have you ever received Jesus Christ as your Savior?" He answered that he had not. Then I asked, "Would you like to receive Him today?" Without hesitation, he answered, "Yes, I would!" He acknowledged that he was a sinner and could not save himself. I told him Jesus had died for his sins, and Dick said he knew that.

Dick and Carol both prayed the sinner's prayer with me that morning. Later, Carol explained that she had prayed that prayer before but had never fully understood what it meant. A year later, they were both baptized.

It has been more than ten years since that situation played out. My precious friend whom I was not allowed to visit died first, and a couple of months later, Carol's aunt died.

"Not being able to understand God is frustrating, but it is ridiculous for us to think we have the right to limit God to something we are capable of comprehending." Francis Chan

I was frustrated with the circumstances that prevented me from seeing my friend but thankfully channeled that frustration into a positive move by visiting an elderly woman from our congregation instead. Out of that decision, God allowed me to lead two people to salvation through His Son, Jesus Christ. God knew ahead what they would need and what I would need.

I will see my precious friend in Heaven, and Carol's aunt also. But more importantly, I will get to see Carol and Dick, two people I got to know because God closed a window and opened a door.

"All the paths of the Lord are mercy and truth, To such as keep His covenant and His testimonies."
Psalms 25:10

CHAPTER NINE

HEART ATTACK

"And the Lord, He is the One who goes before you, He will be with you, He will not leave you or forsake you; do not fear nor be dismayed." Deuteronomy 31:8

"Daddy has had a heart attack." Mum's words were strained as they came across the phone. A couple of hours earlier, she had rushed Dad to the hospital with the emergency lights on the car flashing. He sat beside her, clutching at his chest and struggling to breathe while he urged Mom to run the lights. Upon their arrival, he was taken in for an emergency procedure to place a stent in his artery, but something went wrong during the surgery.

At the hospital, Stan, Mum, and I stared at him lying there in a drug-induced coma. A ventilator tube was taped to his mouth and there was no response when we spoke his name. Machines beeped, IV's dripped, and a nurse hovered nearby. My Dad was a strong, capable man, and quick to help someone in need. But now he was unable to help himself. The whole setting was surreal, and my mind couldn't seem to grasp the seriousness of the situation. The doctors only gave vague updates and made no promises that he would pull through. I struggled to keep my heart out of my head. I wanted to stay strong for Mum, and everything within me fought the urge to collapse into racking sobs.

We asked our churches to pray, family members prayed, and the urgent request passed swiftly from one concerned friend to another. Messages of care came from all over the United States, and we realized our circle of prayer support was growing wider and stronger. My heart was warmed by the support that came flooding in.

Three days went by, and it seemed that things were at a standstill. Dad wasn't failing, but he also wasn't gaining. Each time we went into his room for a short visit, nothing seemed different. Stan and I took turns going in with Mum and she was able to hold herself together while we sat beside his bed, but as soon as we walked away, she was in tears again.

I wondered what God was going to do. Would Dad survive, or would he go to Glory? A strange battle played out inside my mind. I started planning Dad's funeral, but my heart would stop me, telling me not to dig a hole for Dad until he was dead. Even though a battle raged within me, a calming peace flooded my soul – a peace that could only come as a result of the prayers that were being said on our behalf.

On Friday night, the cardiac doctor said he wasn't going to pull Dad out of the coma until Monday. Meanwhile, he was turning Dad's case over to the weekend coverage doctor. We all knew at some point soon Dad would have to be weaned off the drugs or permanent damage would ensue. Dad was approaching that time limit, and Monday seemed awfully far away. We looked at each other with concern, but no one dared to say out loud what our hearts feared. Never had I felt such a sense of waiting – as if my whole being was holding its breath.

I lived thirty miles from the hospital and juggled the care of my family with time to sit with Mum. I drove the distance between my house and the hospital in a stupor, hardly remembering the miles. I don't remember what my family did without me. I only remember the feeling that time was standing still, and we were left waiting. That's it, just waiting.

"The effective, fervent prayer of a righteous man avails much."
James 5:16

On Sunday morning, I went to the hospital to sit with Mum while my brother Stan, a pastor, preached in the first service at his church. His assistant pastor covered the second service, and Stan was at the hospital by 10:30 AM. Mum and I went to get a bite to eat while Stan sat by Dad's bed. A little later we went back into the room, and Stan was sitting close to Dad's bed, intently watching his face. His voice was low and urgent. "The doctor has started pulling Dad out of the coma. He thinks Dad can do it." We looked at each other in amazement. The weekend doctor was doing something we hadn't expected, and in a short time, Dad started stirring. The clock said twelve noon and a powerful thought hit me. Hundreds of Christians had prayed for Dad in their morning worship service. Now, God was moving in answer to those prayers!

Because I was getting over a cold, I stood in the back of the room and purposely stayed away from Dad's face, watching Stan and Mum talk to Dad. He seemed to hear their voices and gain comfort from them. It seemed we were living a dream as the events unfolded before us. I could feel the presence of God in the room, and there was no doubt we were watching a miracle happen right before our eyes. People had prayed, and now God was moving. By evening Dad was conscious, and the ventilator had been removed. His progress was slow but steady, and over time he fully recovered. That amazing event happened fourteen years ago. Thankfully, Dad is still with us today, working hard, and determined to carry on.

"Ultimately, God has the prerogative over our life and death." Jerry Pierce

I have never forgotten that Sunday morning in the ICU when we knew the presence of God was in the room. I still remember looking at the clock on the wall, realizing the significance of the timing, and knowing God was moving among us. I believe God specifically chose that doctor to work on that weekend to pull Dad out of the coma before the drugs could hurt him permanently. God had gone ahead of us, knowing what the coverage schedule had to be for that doctor to be there for Dad. God is always making a way for us, getting things ready for our arrival, and I am thankful we saw it happen clearly that day.

"Where can I go from Your Spirit? Or where can I flee from Your presence? If I ascend into heaven, You are there; If I make my bed in hell, behold, You are there. If I take the wings of the morning, And dwell in uttermost parts of the sea, Even there Your hand shall lead me, And Your right hand shall hold me."
Psalms 139:7-10

CHAPTER TEN

PERFECT TIMING

"For God so loved the world that He gave His only begotten Son, that whoever believes in Him should not perish but have everlasting life." John 3:16

People in town knew Karen as a giving, caring person who would help anyone in need. In addition to working full-time, she volunteered in our town's fire department, belonged to several community causes, and was a terrific single mom to two teenagers. But we all knew she was dying. She had been able to beat back the cancer a few years earlier, but it had returned with a vengeance, and this time Karen was losing the battle.

Everyone loved her warm, selfless personality, but I was afraid that she wouldn't go to Heaven when she died. As wonderful as Karen was, I didn't think she was saved, so I began to pray earnestly that God would allow me to speak to her about her soul.

I drove by her house when I went to town and saw that she often had visitors. How would I ever get a chance to speak to her alone? Although we were acquainted with each other, Karen and I weren't close. I had no idea how I could gracefully walk into her house and announce I was there to talk about death. Who does that to a single mother?

Day after day, I drove by Karen's house and prayed for her soul. Time and time again, I asked God to show me how to approach the subject and when to do it. Two seasons went by and I still hadn't talked to Karen about salvation. I held my breath, wondering if I would get the chance, but didn't have peace about being pushy.

Then one day it happened. My seven-year-old son, Ben, was at a church activity and I found myself free to do something on my own. I prayed, "Lord, what should I do now?" Right away the answer came. "It's time to go see Karen." I called and asked if I could buy sandwiches and have lunch with her. She graciously welcomed the suggestion and agreed on a time. On my way out the door, I grabbed a paperback New Testament.

When I arrived, Karen welcomed me from the couch where she was propped up on pillows. Water, crackers, and medicine had been set within her reach, but she was the only one at home. She was weak, but able to converse while we ate. We talked about her children and her health in general terms. My heart cried out to God for perfect timing to ask Karen about her soul. She half-heartedly nibbled on her sandwich, then commented that she didn't have much of an appetite and asked me to put the leftovers in the refrigerator.

As I settled back down across from her, I asked if I could read from the Bible, and she readily agreed. I opened to John 14 to read a bit from verses 1-6.

"Let not your heart be troubled, you believe in God, believe also in Me. In my Father's house are many mansions; if it were not so, I would have told you. I go to prepare a place for you. And if I go and prepare a place for you, I will come again and receive you to Myself; that where I am, there you may be also." Thomas said to Him, "Lord, we do not know

*where You are going, and how can we know the way?"
Jesus said to him, "I am the way, the truth, and the life.
No one comes to the Father except through Me."*

Karen listened carefully to every word I read. When I looked up from the Bible I asked, "Did you know that you can know for sure you are going to Heaven when you die?" She caught her breath in a small gasp, locked eyes with me, and asked, "I can?" I answered, "Yes. The Bible is clear that we cannot earn our way to Heaven, but Jesus died for our sins and promised that if we will receive Him as our Savior, He will take us to Heaven when we die."

I turned to Romans 3:23 and read, *"For all have sinned and fall short of the glory of God."* Then I read Romans 6:23, *"For the wages of sin is death, but the gift of God is eternal life in Christ Jesus our Lord."*

My heart was pounding, but somehow, I managed to steady my voice to ask, "Karen, do you believe you are a sinner?" Her voice had become stronger since I started asking the hard questions, and she answered, "Oh yes, I know I am a sinner." Courage rose up in my heart as I continued, asking, "Do you realize that you cannot save yourself?" There was no question in her voice as she answered, "Yes, I do."

I pressed on. "Romans 5:8 says, *'God demonstrates His own love toward us, in that while we were still sinners, Christ died for us.'* Do you believe Jesus died for your sins?" Still listening closely, she answered, "Yes, I do!" Finally, I threw out the ultimate question. "You can pray right now and ask Jesus to come into your heart to save you from your sins. Would you like to do that?" I rejoiced as she answered, "Oh yes, I would!"

Karen's voice was clear as she prayed with me, acknowledging that she was a sinner and could not save herself. Then she asked Jesus to come into her heart and save her from her sin. She finished by thanking God for answering her prayer. After that I prayed and thanked God for saving Karen and giving her the assurance that she would go to Heaven when she died.

I was bursting with thanksgiving as I drove away that day. God's timing couldn't have been more perfect. God had prepared the way ahead of me, and Karen was ready, truly wanting to be saved!

"To wait on God means to pause and soberly consider our own inadequacy and the Lord's all-sufficiency, and to seek counsel and help from the Lord, and to hope in Him." **John Piper**

I left the Bible with Karen, but it turned out that she had very little time to read it. A week after our visit, her health took a turn for the worse and her mind became clouded with pain. Three weeks after our visit, Karen went to Heaven to be with Jesus.

On the day of Karen's funeral, the church was packed with people mourning the loss of a wonderful, generous soul. The pastor announced she was following a program for the service that Karen had written a year before. It was then that I understood why she was willing to talk openly about the state of her soul. She was a desperate woman who knew her time was short. God had perfectly prepared her heart for that moment when she would consider His offer to save her. I am thankful that one day I will see her again, and God's timing will be perfect then, too.

The "Romans Road" to Salvation

Romans 3:23 *For all have sinned and fall short of the glory of God.*

Romans 6:23 *For the wages of sin is death, but the free gift of God is eternal life in Christ Jesus our Lord.*

Romans 5:8 *But God shows His love for us in that while we were still sinners, Christ died for us.*

Romans 10:9 *Because, if you confess with your mouth that Jesus is Lord and believe in your heart that God raised Him from the dead, you will be saved.*

Romans 10:13 *For everyone who calls on the name of the Lord will be saved.*

How to pray for salvation:
Dear Jesus, I know I am a sinner and cannot save myself. Thank you for coming to die on the cross for my sins. I pray that you will forgive my sins and come into my heart to live. Thank you for hearing my prayer and for saving me. In Jesus' Name, Amen.

Verses of Assurance

Romans 5:1 *Therefore, since we have been justified by faith, we have peace with God through our Lord Jesus Christ.*

Romans 8:1 *There is therefore no condemnation for those who are in Christ Jesus.*

Romans 8:38-39 *For I am sure that neither death nor life, nor angels, nor rulers, nor things present nor things to come, nor powers, nor height nor depth, nor anything else in all creation, will be able to separate us from the love of God in Christ Jesus our Lord.*

CHAPTER ELEVEN

FORGET ME NOT

"I am with you always..." Matthew 28:20

"I am not a theologian or a scholar, but I am very aware of the fact that pain is necessary to all of us. In my own life, I think I can honestly say that out of the deepest pain has come the strongest conviction of the presence of God and the love of God." Elisabeth Elliot

Sometime between the accident that killed my husband and his funeral I went out to check the mail, and there on the ground beneath the mailbox was a clump of flowers with the roots attached. They were carefully wrapped with a plastic bag around the bottom, as if to keep them safe for replanting. There was no note or other evidence of where they had come from. Although I enjoy gardening, I was in no mood to plant anything. Still, I didn't want to waste the care put into those flowers, so I hastily dug a crude hole in my flower garden and stuck the roots into the ground. Then I pressed the dirt around them and walked away.

Later in the summer, I noticed that even though the blossoms had died off, the plants seemed to have taken root, and I wondered what kind of flowers they were. Exactly one year after Michael died, tiny flowers graced the garden with soft blue blooms. A friend told me they were Forget Me Nots. Since then they have spread, and I have given some away, or transplanted some to other spots. But always a clump of blue appears in the same place I put it during that unforgettable week in 2007.

Forget Me Not. I never discovered who left those lovely flowers below my mailbox, but they are here to remind me every year on that fateful anniversary. While it is true that they do remind me of my husband, they also remind me of all that God has done since that day. I am reminded that He carried me through the early years of trauma, and that He has proven Himself true through many changes. I cannot count the times I have come up against a new situation that took my breath away, only to realize that God was already there, getting things ready for my arrival!

Forget Me Not. I am so thankful for the thoughtful person who left that little bunch of flowers below my mailbox that day - a clump of flowers that comes back every year to remind me again that God never makes mistakes. He is always the same, giving me strength through the darkest days, and the longest nights.

"I am the Lord, I do not change;"
Malachi 3:6

In one second on May 25, 2007, my life changed forever. But God has not changed. He has proven Himself faithful, gently drawing me close to His chest. I am enveloped in His love, always secure in His care, and confident that He is going ahead of me through every unknown twist and turn of this road we call life.

CHAPTER TWELVE

THE PRAYER SHAWL

"I pray for them. I do not pray for the world but for those whom You have given Me, for they are Yours. And all Mine are Yours, and Yours are Mine, and I am glorified in them." John 17:9-10

One Sunday at church, my friend, Mark, met me in the parking lot with a gift bag. "This is from my coworker, Mary. She made it for you." Inside the bag was a beautiful, blue prayer shawl woven in big, fuzzy stitches with lovely fringes on each end. Mark had told Mary about my husband's accident, and a few weeks later she asked Mark to give me the shawl. I was taken aback at her selflessness and sweet generosity. A woman I had never met took the time to make me a prayer shawl. I had never heard of a prayer shawl, but it was precious to me from the start.

At first, I wasn't sure what to do with the shawl, so I draped it over the end of my bed. It was my favorite color and looked lovely with the other hues of blue that decorated the bedroom. But soon that shawl became my dear friend. Since Michael's accident, I had struggled with insomnia and could not put my shattered dreams to sleep. Every night, I played Christian music and crawled into bed hoping for sleep to come, knowing it would probably escape me again. Michael had been a noisy sleeper, and now the quiet bedroom shouted his absence. Even the ticking wall clock seemed to emphasize the empty silence.

One night, I desperately grabbed the prayer shawl, gobbed it into a ball, hugged it to my chest, and sobbed in the darkness. The softness of the shawl against my face and neck seemed to soothe my soul. I fell into a fitful sleep, grateful for the comfort that the shawl gave my anguished soul. For months, I followed the same routine every night. I put on Christian music, hugged the rolled-up shawl, and fell asleep while I prayed.

I thought the prayer shawl was meant to be used when I was praying, and sometimes I did use it for that. Several times, I threw it around my shoulders as I crashed to my knees, desperately sobbing in tormented prayer. Somehow, I found comfort in the shawl's warm embrace.

Over time, I used the shawl less and less. Then I put it away for safekeeping. Once, I almost gave it to someone else who was hurting, but could not bring myself to do it.

"Time spent in prayer is never wasted." Francois Fenelon

A few years ago, my brother, Floyd, was diagnosed with a rare, incurable form of cancer. The news was unbearable, and in my despair, I remembered the shawl. Once again, it became my nightly companion. But I did not need it nearly as long as I had the first time, and after a few weeks, was able to put it back in the closet.

"But I have prayed for you, that your faith should not fail;" Luke 22:32

I recently found out that a prayer shawl is something someone makes while they pray for the recipient. I'm convinced that the woman who made my shawl had a very close connection with God. Who knew that God could use a piece of soft blue knitting to bring profound consolation to my shattered soul?

I have learned a lot from that shawl. I have learned that we do not know what God might use to help others. He might use prayer, a hug, or a kind word. He might use a monetary gift, a ride to the store, or a timely phone call. God can use anything He wants to deliver help to those in need. He can even use a prayer shawl.

God gave that selfless lady the ability to make beautiful shawls a long time before she ever made one for me. He knew that one day she would hear of a brokenhearted widow who needed prayer accompanied by a soft piece of woven yarn. I find it amazing that God, in His awesome way, would direct other people's lives to meet my needs. That prayer shawl illustrates, once again, that God is always ahead of me!

CHAPTER THIRTEEN

OUR ANNIVERSARY

"He who calls you is faithful, who also will do it."
I Thessalonians 5:24

June 11, 1983 is a date that will never go unnoticed in our family because it was the day that Michael and I got married. We were married two weeks short of twenty-four years. Someone asked if that is a sad day for me. The answer is yes... and no.

Yes, because it makes me pause and wonder what life would have been like as a couple in this stage of life. Yes, because life is much harder without a husband to share the load. But no, because I have so much to be thankful for. Through that marriage, God gave me four wonderful people - two daughters and two sons.

I am thankful that all of Michael's children remember him, and that we have funny stories to tell about his quirks and habits. We compare each of his sons and daughters to him and note which person inherited which characteristic. A couple of them got his athletic abilities, all of them got his great intelligence, and one of them inherited his lack of musical ability. When we sit around making those comparisons, we smile.

Still, I wish he could be here to share hunting stories with our younger son, Ben. I wish he could be here to talk about computers and work-related issues with his namesake, Mike Jr. I wish he could be here to congratulate our firstborn daughter, Sarah, and her husband, Jon, on the wise decisions they are making in life. Sarah married a man so much like her father, and I know that Michael and Jon would have greatly enjoyed each other's company. I wish Michael could hear the beautiful music that our daughter, Stephanie, and her husband, Andrew, make together. I wish I could see him playing with all of his grandchildren.

"Though you have changed a thousand times, He has not changed once." Charles Spurgeon

In all of my musings, I am reminded that things change and people change. Life without Michael has brought more changes than I could have ever imagined. I am not the same person I was when Michael was killed. But would I want to be? I have grown in skills and abilities, but more importantly, I have grown spiritually. I have learned to depend on God during my darkest days and longest nights. Even as I have seen many ways that God has gone ahead of me, I am sure that there are many more that I won't see until I get to Heaven.

So yes, my wedding anniversary does bring memories and musings. But it also brings with it an attitude of thanksgiving that only comes from going through the depths of grief and coming out on the other side. I know that I have been carried by the Almighty, and HE is faithful!

"Let us hold fast the confession of our hope without wavering, for He who promised is faithful."
Hebrews 10:23

CHAPTER FOURTEEN

HIS BIRTHDAY

"I will never leave you or forsake you." Hebrews 13:5

Ten months after Michael was killed, my family had one last painful hurdle to climb over in the first year of our loss. It was his birthday on April 4th.

Birthdays were a big deal for our family. The birthday guy or girl could request a special meal, including their choice of cake and frosting flavors. There were gifts to be opened and photos to be taken of the birthday person's big day. But with Michael gone, his birthday took on a different meaning, and we wondered what we should do. Should we mourn? Should we light memorial candles? As crazy as it sounded, I suggested that we go out to supper and celebrate the day that Michael was born. After all, nothing would have been the same for us if he hadn't been born.

Sarah turned twenty-three two months after her dad died, and had taken a job as the general manager for Tim Horton's in Bangor. She woke up that morning with the heartbreaking knowledge that, for the first time in her life, she would go through her father's birthday without him. Arriving at work, she discovered that an employee had called in sick unexpectedly, and no one was available to cover the spot. Business was unusually busy that day, and Sarah hurried to cover her own position and the empty one, too.

At lunchtime, an employee named Jason went out back to take his fifteen-minute break. He wasn't supposed to leave the property during his break, but his sister needed a ride somewhere, and he was sure he could drop her off and return in under fifteen minutes. So, he hurried out the back door without telling Sarah.

People were hungry and the ordering line was almost out the door when someone told Sarah she had a phone call. Without looking up from making sandwiches, she responded, "Take a message, I can't come to the phone." The employee replied, "It's Jason." Sarah stopped, blinked, and asked, "Jason? Isn't he out back?" She picked up the phone to hear Jason say he had been in a fender-bender and couldn't come back to work until he filed a police report. She hurried back to the front, trying to figure out how to cover three vacant positions.

Just then, an elderly gentleman tripped on a large floor mat as he came through the door and landed face-down on the floor. People surrounded him to see if he was all right and he stood up with a bloody lip, obviously embarrassed at making a scene. Sarah went around the counter to ask if he was okay, but he seemed anxious to forget the whole thing so that people would stop looking at him. He ordered his food and hurried out the door, but another customer jumped the line and confronted Sarah. "You can't just let him go. You have to get his name, and find out if he's all right!" Sarah grabbed a piece of paper and dashed out the door to find the gentleman. She took his name and number, and he told her once again that he was okay. She ran back inside to find a line of customers impatiently waiting for their orders.

Later that afternoon when things had quieted down, Sarah's boss, Jamie, came in to see how her day was going. She fed him the many incidents of the day in small chunks. Somehow, Jamie knew there was something she wasn't telling him, and after each report he asked, "And what else?" Jamie is a kind man and perceived that Sarah was upset about more than a hectic day at the store, so he asked again, "And what else?" She looked up from her paperwork with hurt in her eyes and whispered, "Today is Dad's birthday."

"The Lord is near to those who have a broken heart, and saves such as are crushed in Spirit." Psalm 34:18

Sarah related the events of her day to us while we ate supper that night, and we sympathized with her that it was a lousy day for everything to go wrong. I would love to tell you that the rest of the evening was frivolous and filled with mindless hilarity, but it wasn't. Although we did talk about many different things, we did not talk much about Michael. In some ways, it was like ignoring the elephant in the room. After all, we already knew the obvious — we were here without him. His absence said everything that needed to be said. Frankly, when the day was over, I was glad that we had gotten through it without many tears.

I have never regretted choosing that method to remember Michael's birthday. Time has lessened the pain, and now April 4th isn't nearly as painful as it used to be. God is still faithful every day. We have walked this road of loss for many years, and we never could have made it without God carrying us through this deep, dark valley called Death. He gives peace, comfort, and strength through horrifyingly hard circumstances. When the days are dark and the nights are long, He is still here.

I have found God to be nearer and sweeter since Michael's death. He has promised never to leave us or forsake us, and He has kept that promise. He has promised that when we walk through fire or flood, He will be with us. God always keeps His promises.

Now I walk forward in life with confidence. When hard times come – and they will – I know He will hold me. What I have learned from the past, I carry into the future. One major thing I carry daily, is that God is walking ahead of me and He will always have things ready for my arrival. The same God who didn't leave me helpless yesterday will certainly be there to help me in all of my tomorrows.

"There is more safety with Christ in the tempest than without Christ in the calmest waters."
Alexander Grosse

CHAPTER FIFTEEN

THE CAR

"The Lord is good to those who wait for Him, to the soul who seeks Him." Lamentations 3:7

A couple of years after Michael died, the mechanics in my family, my brothers and father, began urging me to look for a new car because mine was starting to need more repairs than it was worth. I had never bought a car before and the thought of doing it left me utterly paralyzed by fear. Before I was married, my father always made sure I had a good vehicle, and Michael had taken care of our car purchases after we were married. I was sure I would make a mistake and buy a lemon, or for one reason or another, regret my purchase a few thousand miles down the road. I started praying that God would direct my path, and that I wouldn't buy the wrong vehicle.

I purchased a Consumer Reports and poured over the pages. At first the words seemed to be written in a foreign language, because I didn't understand the categories, charts, or classes the cars were divided into. Mike Jr. loved cars and helped me sort out the pros and cons of different-sized vehicles. I learned the meaning of new words like make, model, options, packages, and miles per gallon. I knew I wanted a vehicle big enough to tow a camper, so I learned about the length of a wheel base, turning radius, and towing capacity. I put markers on different pages of the Consumer Reports and flipped through it back and forth, making comparisons until that magazine became ragged.

I made a mental list of what I wanted in a vehicle. I wanted something large enough to tow a mid-size camper, although I didn't have a camper. (Try telling a sales person that you need a car with a towing package, because you're going to tow a camper. Then when they ask you what size your camper is, watch their face when you tell them that you don't have a camper.)

Despite all I was learning, I couldn't get past how intimidated I was about making such a big choice. I grew up working around cars, and hearing the respect in my father's voice about their value. Many times, he said,

"Next to buying a house, a vehicle is the largest purchase a person will ever make." I felt terribly unqualified for such a huge decision. When fear climbed up through my chest and clutched at my throat, I would toss the Consumer Reports into a corner and walk away. Sometimes a month would go by before I mustered up enough courage to look at it again.

The vehicle I owned was still road-worthy, so I had time to think and pray about my next car. Occasionally I would go to a dealership and look at their vehicles. I wanted something new, because I didn't want to worry about a used one breaking down soon after the purchase. But I didn't want to pay a new price, so that greatly limited my options. Did I mention I was praying?

Several times I tried different vehicles, but when I asked God if that was the one I should buy, I just felt like His response was, "You have to wait."

"I will instruct you and teach you in the way you should go; I will guide you with My eye." Psalm 32:8

Mike Jr. loves new cars and was quite annoyed by my indecisiveness, especially since I wasn't shopping nearly as hard as he thought I should be. A typical conversation with him would be, "Mom! You won't find a car to buy if you don't look at cars!" "Mike, what I want is for God to drop a car into my yard and say, 'There you go. That's your car, now buy it.'" "Mom, you know that's not how it works!" Mike's impatience with me didn't help me find a car, but it did increase my angst.

For starters, I wanted everyone in my car to be comfortable, so I always sat in the back seat to make sure it felt good. At one dealership I commented to a sales man that the back seats seemed uncomfortable in the car I had just tried. He snorted and said it was a good thing that I was riding in the driver's seat! That man didn't hear from me again.

Finally, on a cool fall day I tried out a car at a local dealership. I liked the way it felt, but that model didn't have a towing package. The salesman's name was Tiffan, and he made a great impression on me. First of all, he was a big, tall man with kindly eyes and a friendly manner. Second, he was detailed and attentive but not pushy. I really liked him. Tiffan said he had a car in New Hampshire just like the one I had tried, and came with a towing package. If I would pay him $500 and sign a contract saying I would buy it, he would go get it for me. More of my Dad's advice marched through my head, "Never buy a car in the dark, sight unseen." I told Tiffan I would pray about it and let him know.

When I told Mike Jr. about that conversation he exclaimed, "I bet I can find that car on the internet!" And, true to his nature, he did. "Look, Mom! That's the car! That's the one Tiffan wants to sell you!" Sure enough, it looked exactly like what Tiffan had described, and it was located in Concord, NH. But it was more money than I wanted to spend. I asked God if I should go to New Hampshire and look at that car, but again God responded, "You need to wait."

"God plans to use the long pauses in our lives for our blessing . . . if we let Him." Dr. Charles Stanley

Winter arrived with the holidays, and I put the burden of choosing a different car on the back burner. I needed to block that out of my mind, and happily, I was able to.

In January, I was scheduled to take my Verbal Communication Class to Concord, NH for a speech competition. I asked the Lord if I should go look at that car, and felt like He okayed it.

I called Tiffan to ask if that car was still available, and if he would give me the address for the dealership. He said it was, gave me the address, and then paused. "You do know that they will try to sell you the car right there, right?" "Yes, but surely by now you know that I'm not an easy sell," I replied. Relief filled his voice as he answered, "Yes, I do know that."

Our dear friends, Jim and Sandal, live in Concord, and Ben and I stayed with them during the speech competition. On Saturday, we planned to go look at the car, so I asked Jim if he would go with us. I liked it right away, but let Jim drive it first. "Now, Jim, your job is to tell me why I shouldn't buy this car." Jim couldn't find anything wrong with it, and when I drove it, everything felt just right. I finally had hope that I found the right car.

I knew I wouldn't buy it in New Hampshire because that wouldn't be fair to Tiffan, but I wondered how I could honestly address the salesman in Concord. Back at the dealership we sat down with the salesman and I said, "I really like that car. What do you want to tell me?" His eyes were eager, "Chrysler is introducing a whole new set of incentives, and they should be unrolled by Tuesday. Come back then, and I can give you all the details." Wonderful! I was so relieved that I could honestly walk away from the sale without seeming unkind to that man.

On Monday morning, I called Tiffan. "Tiffan, I tried out that car in Concord this weekend, and I really like it. What do you want to tell me?" He sounded excited. "Chrysler is introducing a whole new set of incentives, and they should be out tomorrow. I will call you back as soon as I get the details."

Chrysler's incentives for the previous years' models were huge: Below employee pricing, 0% financing, and they agreed to add a 100,000-mile bumper-to-bumper warranty for a small fee. God had finally put the right car right in front of me!

I was thrilled beyond measure because God had led me to the right car. While I was learning to wait on His timing,

He was holding the perfect vehicle for me. The day that we test-drove it in Concord, the odometer read 38 miles. Either nobody else wanted a family car with a towing package, or God just made everyone else blind while He held it for me.

As I write this chapter, that same car is sitting in my driveway with 238,000 miles on it. I have loved every mile, and God has kept it running in terrific condition.

The biggest lesson I have learned since Michael died is to wait on God. I know I am not the only person who struggles with patience. I find myself pacing while I'm on hold on the phone; I have been known to complain that the 'fast food' isn't coming fast enough; and yes, I have even impatiently wondered why a pot of water doesn't come to a boil faster. Yet, waiting on God has been such a valuable lesson for me. It has provided for me in many ways, and I am thankful that while I have waited on Him, He has gone ahead of me, getting things ready for my arrival!

CHAPTER SIXTEEN

WAIT

"Wait for the Lord; be strong, and let your heart take courage; wait for the Lord!" Psalm 27:14

Our family has had a long tradition of camping, including a much-anticipated annual trip to Canada. When Michael died, I sold our large, older camper because he had always done the towing and I knew I needed a smaller, lighter one.

The summer that Michael died, I rented a camper that was delivered to our vacation lot in Canada. The second year, we didn't go because of sickness in the family. The third year, a friend insisted that we take her pop-up camper because she wasn't going to need it. That was my first experience towing, and I knew from watching Michael that backing up while towing was tricky business, so I was careful not to get myself into a situation where I would have to do that.

In the meantime, I kept shopping for a camper to take the place of the one I had sold. No matter where I went or what I looked at, nothing seemed to be the right fit for me. Either it was the wrong camper, or it was the right one but the wrong price.

As the years went by, I found myself repeating the same shopping process. I would stop at a dealership, look at different models and ask questions, but I couldn't find the right recreational vehicle. I managed to learn a lot about campers through that process, and decided that there were four features that stood out as must-haves for my next camper. I wanted one with ceiling vents that I could open manually, more windows than most of the current models offered, and light-colored interior walls because I need light. Lastly, I knew I needed to have a slide-out room that would provide space for my adult children to visit.

These features seemed to significantly limit my choices in a camper. Whenever I looked at one and prayed for wisdom about buying it, the answer I always felt He gave me was, "You need to wait."

Four years after Michael died, as summer drew near, I prayed more fervently for a camper. Occasionally, I found one at a dealership that came close to what I wanted, and I would pray, "God, do you want me to buy this one?" Still, all I got for an answer was, "You need to wait."

The annual family camping trip was in July. June came and still, there was no RV in my yard. I investigated renting one, but there was nothing suitable in our area. The company that had provided a rental four years earlier was no longer offering that service. I began praying more fervently, "Lord, I pray that You will give me a camper! Please answer the desire of my heart--light walls, lots of windows, manual ceiling vents, and a slide-out." Daily, I cried out to my Heavenly Father with that specific request. I didn't want to skip the annual trip and was disappointed to think that I might have to simply for lack of a place to stay.

I watched for campers for sale by the road, and occasionally stopped to look at one. Still nothing seemed right, and I kept getting the 'wait' signal from God. As the date of our reservations drew closer, my prayers became increasingly urgent.

One day my Dad called, saying that he had gone through a local swap-and-sell publication and had found a few campers for me to call about. Two of the ads seemed promising, so I called about both. One of the owners sent me pictures of her camper that showed light walls, plenty of windows and a slide-out. I became cautiously hopeful about that prospect.

I also discovered that a second camper Dad told me about was only five miles from the first one. I doubted my ability to choose a good camper over an undesirable one, so I called my friend, Jim. After Michael died, Jim did much to help our family, and he agreed to help me again by coming to look at both units. Since they were in a town 150 miles from my house, I made appointments to see both on the same day.

"Lead me in Your truth and teach me, for You are the God of my salvation; On You I wait all the day." Psalm 25:5

On the appointed day, I drove to an immaculate property where the first unit was set up. As the owners led me up the steps and into the camper, I caught my breath in joy. Silently I prayed, "Oh God, are you going to give me a camper that is THIS beautiful?" It had a big slide-out, lovely, light-colored walls, ceiling vents, and plenty of windows. My heart jumped at the beauty and specific answer to my prayers. We talked about the features and specifications, but I tried not to show too much enthusiasm because I didn't know what the other travel trailer was like. I told them we were going to look at the other one and I would let them know what I decided.

The second camper was disappointing for several reasons. It was dark, didn't have a slide-out, and it didn't look as attractive as the advertiser's pictures had led me to believe. While we were looking at it, the owner struggled to keep one of the cupboards from falling apart. Jim stood there for several minutes trying to help the man fix it. I was unimpressed with the condition of that unit and couldn't get the images of the other camper out of my mind.

Driving away, I knew for sure that I wanted the first camper. Excitement built within me, and I allowed myself to be cautiously optimistic that I might have found the one I had been waiting for. Only one problem remained—the asking price was slightly more than what I had budgeted. I called the owners and asked if we could come talk with them again.

They welcomed us into their home to have a friendly conversation about money. We sat in their living room and had the most comfortable dickering conversation I have ever had. In the end, they lowered the price to exactly what I had budgeted, and even offered to deliver the camper to my house, which was a tremendous blessing to me because I hadn't brought the hitch and other towing gear with me. Besides, I had never towed anything except that little pop-up camper I used the year before.

"God always gives His best to those who leave the choice to Him." Jim Elliot

It was a two-and-a-half-hour drive home, and I didn't stop smiling for at least the first hour of the trip. My heart flooded with the goodness of God and I couldn't stop chuckling. I kept praising and thanking Him repeatedly for His overwhelming generosity. He knew the desires of my heart and had set up the perfect camper with perfect features for the perfect purchase price. That camper had only been for sale for a month. If I had jumped ahead of God and bought another one that was not in my budget, or one that did not have the features I had wanted, I would have missed out on the ideal unit that God had for me. Not only that, but Jim had been scheduled to go to Canada with his wife that weekend, but because of sickness they had not gone. Jim drove an hour-and-a-half to help me shop on a weekend when he wasn't supposed to be available. The timing could not have been more perfect!

When the sellers delivered the camper, they explained how everything worked, and patiently waited while I took copious notes. It was like buying from friends.

Learning to Tow

Our annual camping trip to Canada was only two weeks away. Within a few days of the delivery, I hooked up the camper and towed it to my parents' house, which was an hour away. They have a big, flat field behind their house, which was perfect for my towing lesson. Dad put up orange cones and taught me how to back it up and how to take wide turns.

It would be better stated that he "tried" to teach me. Ben was watching from a safe distance and found my driving lesson to be hilarious. We lost count of how many times I hit the orange cones, and Ben was laughing so hard that he fell over on the ground. My father became so frustrated that he told me to keep working on it and walked away. I practiced until my brain hurt and could no longer distinguish left from right. Finally, I gained a marginal amount of confidence and drove home.

Just two days before we were supposed to leave for Canada, we visited with our friends, Bill and Elizabeth, whom I had not seen in years. They inquired about our upcoming trip, and Elizabeth expressed that she had always wanted to go to that spot in Canada. On the spur of the moment, I invited her to go with us, and to my delight, she accepted.

Two days later, even though I had only towed the camper once before, I hooked it up and drove 350 miles to our annual vacation spot. My hands cramped from holding the steering wheel too tightly, and I caught myself holding my breath when I came to a tight spot in the road. But

Elizabeth complimented my driving and kept me distracted during the long ride. Despite my poor driving in Dad's field, somehow, I maneuvered through tight construction zones and over narrow roads to the safety of our destination. I wonder if I would have done that well if God had not given her to me for encouragement.

Once again, it's easy to see how God was going ahead of me with the camper purchase. To this day I love that RV, and when I walk through it, I thank God that He has taught me to wait.

Waiting in this modern world is hard to do. We get irritated if the internet is slow, or if our food isn't ready when we pull up to the drive-thru window. When David was praying, he said, "I will wait on you, Lord." I am thankful that God has lovingly taught me to wait on Him for answers to life's decisions, both great and small. His timing is perfect, and I know I can trust Him.

CHAPTER SEVENTEEN

COFFEE

"...for you yourselves are taught by God to love one another." I Thessalonians 4:9

Early one Saturday morning, I was on my way to speak at a ladies' conference and decided to stop for a cup of coffee to ward off my sleepiness. I knew there was a gas station that served coffee a few miles ahead, and I decided I would stop there. Right away, I felt the Lord compelling me to stop at the Irving Convenience Store instead. I thought, "No. I'll go to that other one. They have good coffee." Once again, I felt a strong push from the Lord to stop at the Irving. In my head, I argued with God. WHY do I argue with God? The Irving was coming up on the left, and if I was going to stop there, I would need to change lanes. Despite my hesitation, I could sense the Lord urging me firmly and clearly to stop at the Irving. I put on my blinker and pulled into the turning lane.

Inside the Irving, there was a smorgasbord of coffees to choose from. I got a cup and stood in front of the self-serve counter, not wanting to cut in front of the woman standing there with two cups in her hand. She carefully studied the names of the flavors and was obviously struggling with the choices.

"There's a lot to choose from, isn't there?" I commented to her. "Yes," she replied, "and I'm getting one for my wife. She's picky about her coffee!"

People in Maine love to talk about their coffee, so we discussed the different flavors, and whether the strong coffee tastes better than the milder blend. The cashier wasn't busy and leaned over the counter to offer her opinion as to the best coffee flavor. Finally, the woman standing next to me chose coffee for her wife, and then for herself. Then I filled my cup with my favorite flavor.

After we had each made our selections, we moved to another counter to add cream and sugar. The friendly banter continued between us about small print on the creamers, and the need for reading glasses. We both agreed that we couldn't read fine print like we used to. That spot in the store would ordinarily be bustling with people trying to get their morning brew, but on this morning, it was just the two of us.

She was a friendly lady, and asked if I was from the area. I told her where I lived, and then asked her if she was from around here. She said she had grown up here but didn't live in-state anymore. She said she was back because her dad had died the day before. I was surprised by her casual statement, and caught my breath in a quiet gasp. My eyes instantly switched off the coffee I was stirring and onto her face. Shock and horror filled my voice as I said, "Oh, I am SO sorry!" She said it was okay, that he had been sick for a while and it had been difficult to watch him under hospice care. Her voice was resigned to his death, and it was clear that she felt that the better thing had happened.

I continued to stir my coffee, suddenly aware of the prompting of God in my heart. This woman needed prayer, and I felt the Lord nudging me to pray for her while we were standing there. But I argued with Him that I didn't have to pray here. Instead, I could just tell her that I would pray for her today. But no, I felt that God wanted me to pray now!

"What's your name?" I asked. "Lisa," she said. I jumped into the next sentence before I could lose courage. "Lisa, would you mind if I prayed for you right now?" To my great relief, she welcomed the idea, saying, "Oh, yes, go right ahead!"

I leaned toward her a little, careful not to overwhelm her personal space. I wondered how to pray, but in faith I said, "Dear Heavenly Father," and I trusted the Lord to guide me. He did guide me to pray for Lisa's comfort and strength in the days to come. I also prayed for help for her whole family. When I said, "Amen," and lifted my eyes, I saw that she had bowed her head and had leaned in toward me, listening intently to every word. The area had stayed quiet, and I think the cashier witnessed every word of the entire exchange.

We said goodbye. I paid the kind cashier for my coffee and headed for the car. As I drove away, I was overwhelmed with awe at God's direction! My heart was filled with wonder as I realized that the need to stop at Irving had nothing to do with my preference for a certain kind of coffee, but had everything to do with a brokenhearted woman who needed prayer!

I continued to pray for Lisa that day, and I have prayed for her several times since then. In retrospect, I wonder if she had encountered hard times and whether the days ahead of her were going to be difficult. Maybe someone was praying that she would meet a Christian who would show her Christ's love? Maybe a family member was asking God to send someone who would witness to her? I don't know the answers to those questions, but I do know that God told His people in Isaiah 30:21, ***"Your ears shall hear a word behind you, saying, 'This is the way, walk in it,' Whenever you turn to the right hand or whenever you turn to the left."*** I know for sure that I was supposed to be in a specific place at a certain time on that particular morning. Although I had argued with God about which place to stop for coffee, His guiding hand put me right where He wanted me.

While I was driving that morning, I was concentrating on the ladies' conference and the different topics that I would be speaking on. I asked God to go ahead of me and prepare the ladies' hearts to receive a blessing at the conference, and He did do that. But before I could arrive at the church, God had already gone ahead of me for a stop that I hadn't planned on. Sometimes God's hand goes ahead of us in wonderfully unexpected ways, if only we're willing to follow His guidance!

"As Christians we live to be the hands and feet of Jesus, called to represent Jesus Christ to a hurting and struggling world. People are watching, people have to know we care." Carl Crouse

CHAPTER EIGHTEEN

LEAKY PIPES AND FROZEN DOORS – PART ONE

"But I will sing of Your power; yes, I will sing aloud of Your mercy in the morning; For You have been my defense and refuge in the day of my trouble."
Psalm 59:16

Winters in Maine tend to be cold, and the 2017- 2018 season was no exception. Most of the state recorded temperatures that stayed below thirty-two degrees for over forty days. The duration of this cold snap broke a thirty-five-year-old record. Adding insult to injury, a 'snow bomb cyclone' was in the forecast for the first week of January. It did not disappoint.

Snow was blowing sideways and piling up fast on the morning of January 4th. Though much of the state was shut down because of the storm, Ben was required to work. At 6:00 AM we hugged goodbye, but he paused with his hand on the doorknob. "What is that sound?" he asked. His voice was filled with alarm as he said, "Something's dripping!" Turning on the living room light, we were shocked to see water dripping out of the ceiling light fixture. Ben bounded upstairs to find the source while I ran downstairs for a bucket. He met me back in the living room with no answers.

I dropped the bucket under the light fixture, raced up over the stairs, and yanked open the attic access door. Sure enough, water was flowing across the plywood floor, seeping through the seams to the ceiling below, and leaking into the electric box that housed the wiring to the ceiling light. The heating pipes on the second-floor wind in and out of the attic, and a broken pipe inside the attic door was slowly streaming water to the room below.

"Mom, I have to go!" Ben gave me another desperate hug and bolted out into the dark, bracing himself against the blast of blowing snow.

Water was splashing around the bucket in the living room and I grabbed a few towels to catch the drops. I noticed that another place on the ceiling had started dripping and threw a towel under that spot too.

Dashing down the basement stairs, I desperately stared at the series of copper tubes winding above the furnace, hoping to find answers. A hot-water baseboard heating system consists of a series of valves and pipes, and I quickly realized I had no idea which pipes fed what. Ben had turned a couple of valves before he left, but neither of us completely understood the system.

It was 6:10 AM, and I knew that because of the blizzard there was a good chance that my early-rising brother was home. He picked up the phone on the third ring. I said, "Stan, I'm sorry to bother you, but I have water dripping out of my living room ceiling light, and I'm pretty sure it's coming from a broken pipe in the attic. Can you tell me which valves to turn off?" His sleepy voice became urgent, "Okay, I'm trying to remember how we set that up." He had installed my heating system twenty years earlier, and the details were fuzzy.

While we discussed pipes, valves, inlets, and outlets I lost my way in his technical descriptions. "Can you FaceTime me?" He pulled the phone away from his face to ask his wife, "Emily, can you FaceTime Linda?" Then, back to me, he stated, "Emily is going to call you."

Through the wonder of modern technology, Stan looked at the hot water boiler in my basement. Talking me through the maze of pipes and valves, he explained which ones to turn off. After several minutes of guiding me through the system, he sighed with relief, "Okay, now the water should quit feeding through that broken pipe."

I thanked him and went back upstairs to see that water had appeared in other spots on the wooden living room floor. The furnace was off, so I considered my other heating options while throwing more towels on the floor. I didn't know when the broken pipe could be fixed, but it certainly wouldn't be during this blizzard.

Alternate Heat

A wonderfully warm fire was already burning in the trusty basement wood stove that had been my constant companion through the winter months. Heat from the stove radiated up into the first floor of my house. However, I was dependent on the furnace to heat the second floor and I sure didn't want any more pipes to freeze. I scrambled to assemble kindling and paper, and soon a cozy fire was crackling in the living room wood stove.

Daylight dawned to reveal that the blowing, drifting snow was causing near white-out conditions. Ben's tire tracks were already disappearing in the swirling drifts. There was no way I would get the broken pipe repaired today. I was on my own, but not alone. Times like this test my faith to the limit. Panic pushes up into my throat threatening to choke me, but I have learned to force it back down by repeating faith-filled facts. "I am not alone. God has not forsaken me. He will give me wisdom and knowledge. I am not alone. I am not alone."

Despite high winds, the power had not gone out, so I made a cup of coffee. The rich aroma wafted through the kitchen and filled my heart with hope. I took a few deep breaths and slowly sipped the soothing liquid. God would help me and show me what to do. I knew He wouldn't fail me.

In anticipation of the blizzard, I had stocked up on wood for the big stove but hadn't brought in extra for the smaller living room stove. Around noon, I bundled up tight while giving thanks for snow pants, boots, a heavy coat, thick hat, and warm mittens. Using a snow shovel that we stored by the cellar door, I was able to clear the doorway that was blocked with snow and trudge toward the wood pile. The sharp wind caught my breath, and I pulled the hat closer to my face against the biting snow. Miraculously, most of the area near the woodpile was blown clear. I made several trips into the cellar with arm loads of wood while thanking God that my shoulders didn't hurt like they had in the past. A lifetime in Maine has taught me that there is always something to be thankful for.

"God is true. His Word of Promise is sure. In all His relations with His people God is faithful. He may be safely relied upon." A.W. Pink

Drops kept appearing on my living room ceiling all day. When one spot seemed to dry up another would appear. Towels were all over the wooden floor, and I emptied the bucket every hour or so. Evening came, and I was worn ragged from a day full of running up and down stairs, lugging wood, and tending two wood stoves. I wanted to go to bed, but new spots kept appearing and I didn't want the living room floor to be ruined with water left on it overnight. So, I sat on the couch listening to the soft plop of water landing on the towels and splatting into the bucket. I considered the damage being done to the ceiling and compared that to problems other people have faced. My house wasn't swept down a river in a hurricane, it wasn't flattened by a wild fire, and it wasn't destroyed by a tornado. I had plenty of heat even though the furnace was off, and the power had not gone out despite the high winds.

I was thankful but wanted to go to bed. Apparently, it takes water a long time to find its way through all the crevices in a ceiling. It seemed most of the spots had dried up except one particularly wet place that continued to drip with gusto. A friend told me to make a hole in the ceiling to let the water out, so I stood on a step ladder and drove a knife up into that stubborn soggy spot. Sure enough, water came pouring out into the bucket I had positioned below. Then it stopped. It had been sixteen hours since we first saw water coming out of the light fixture, and finally it had stopped. Relief washed over me, and I went to bed.

"I will say of the Lord, He is my refuge and my fortress; My God, in Him I will trust." Psalm 91:2

A couple of days later, Ben replaced the broken section of pipe and we followed Stan's instructions to refill the pipes, but nothing happened. Water didn't fill the upstairs pipes, and the heat didn't come. Over the phone, Stan's voice was filled with regret as he said, "I hate to tell you this, but you have another leak."

My heart sank, and I forced myself up over the stairs to systematically empty out the other attic crawl spaces, dreading what I might find in the dark recesses of my house. I needed to access all the pipes so I could rip the insulation off them and find the leak. What other ceiling would be ruined? Hours later, the bedrooms were full of keepsakes and forgotten items from years gone by, but I had not found another leak. "Well, I will have to come down there," Stan said. He has a family and runs a heating business while serving as a full-time pastor. Not only is he a busy man, but Stan also lives quite a distance from me, and I try to avoid asking him for help. Still, he always comes without a single complaint.

Stan's analysis left him puzzled. He couldn't figure out why water wasn't flowing through the system. He found a safety release valve that was malfunctioning and started to change it. "Wait, what is this?" He held out a ball of metal about the size of a small green pea, and said, "This shouldn't have been in that valve. It could be why your lines weren't filling." After making a few more adjustments, Stan turned on the valves and we heard water flowing into the lines. I ran upstairs to see if any of the bare attic pipes were leaking, but they were dry. Stan exclaimed, "Your attic would have been flooded if that ball of metal hadn't been blocking the water line!"

My mind could hardly comprehend his discovery. The water dripping from my ceiling on the day of the blizzard would have been a gushing flood if that line had not been blocked. A couple of weeks later, a carpenter came to replace the Living Room ceiling and when he pulled the insulation out of the rafters, more water from the broken pipe poured onto the floor. God went ahead of me by allowing a small bead of metal to get into that water line, and I have no idea when He did it. His ways are past our comprehension, but they are always perfect!

CHAPTER NINETEEN

LEAKY PIPES AND FROZEN DOORS – PART TWO

"When you pass through the waters, I will be with you;
and through the rivers, they shall not overwhelm you;
when you walk through the fire you shall not be burned,
and the flame shall not consume you." Isaiah 43:2

The morning after we discovered the leak from a pipe that broke during the blizzard, I awoke to over a foot of dense snow in the driveway. Thankfully, the wind had died down and the temperature was rising into the high teens, but it was an effort to wade through the three-foot drift between the house and the garage. The snow was banked hard against the garage door, so I started the ten-horse snow blower by the open door and blew a path through the middle of the driveway. The wind had piled drifts of snow in various places, and it was a trick to coax the snow blower through another three-foot drift in the middle of the driveway. Experience has taught me that the first pass will be the hardest because the scoop of the snow blower is full. After that, I know I can take a half-scoop with each pass.

The end of the driveway was blocked with giant boulders of snow piled four feet high by the town snowplow. After a couple of hours, I went inside to dry my clothes and take a breather. Then I went back out to keep working. It was a satisfying sight to watch the snow fly up out of the chute and land twenty feet away.

By late afternoon I didn't feel like working any more, but knew I couldn't leave fourteen inches of wet snow on the deck. Besides, the forecast for the next day predicted a high temperature of zero degrees, and I didn't want to work in that. I resigned myself to the task, grabbed the snow shovel, and started in. After an hour of pushing and throwing heavy snow, I was totally spent and made a bargain with myself. If I left a few piles of snow in various spots on the deck, I could finish the job in short order tomorrow, and my deck wouldn't be overloaded with weight through the night. Besides, my legs, arms, and back were complaining about the long day of work.

Relieved to have most of the job done, I contemplated my Friday evening options. There was a game at church that night, and I knew I should go visit with other Christians for a while. Ben was working over the weekend and wouldn't be home until Monday, so I needed the company.

Going Out

I took a quick shower and put on jeans, a turtle-neck shirt, and short fashion boots. The dog, Jake, needed to go out. I knew he wouldn't stay out long in the frigid cold, so I didn't put his coat on him. Instead, I quickly hooked him up on his lead by the back door and went back into the bedroom to finish my make-up. A few minutes later, Jake barked, and I hurried to let him in so he wouldn't get too cold. Looking out the door, I saw that he had wrapped his lead around one of the dense piles of snow in the middle of the deck. Disgusted with his innate ability to get his lead wrapped around anything available, I stepped out onto the deck to unwrap it. The storm door slammed behind me as I hurried to free the dog so we could both get back inside. I quickly unwrapped the lead, unhooked the dog from it, and bolted toward the door. Reaching for the cold metal, I pushed on the knob to open the door and was horrified to find it was frozen solid. I banged on it with my fist, but nothing happened. Jake and I were both locked out without our coats on!

I had one key hidden, but it was on the other side of the house. "Come on, Jake," I urged, and plunged my legs into the snow beside the house. Thankfully, it hadn't drifted on that side of the house, so it was only a foot deep. Jake followed in my path, plowing his way through the snow. The biting cold cut through my shirt, and I started shivering. Stepping over the last drift, I ran down the freshly-shoveled walk and hurried to get the key. My hands were shaking with cold as I shoved it into the lock, but was shocked to find that it would only go in a little way. The lock was frozen, something that had never happened before.

Jake stood there expectantly, waiting for me to let him in. I had only been outside for a couple of minutes and was amazed at how cold I had become in such a short time. I knew that neither Jake, nor I would last long outside in the four-degree weather. I tried not to panic as I considered my dwindling options. I found a light, small fleece blanket in the car and hurried to wrap it around my shoulders.

My only hope was that my next-door neighbor, Karen, was home. She liked Jake, and I knew she would let him into her house. "Come on, Jake!" I called and started running down the driveway toward the neighbor's house. It was only 5:00 PM, but the sky was already pitch black. The cold air bit my face while I struggled to see the road. Jake's eyesight isn't what it used to be, and he followed the sound of my running feet. Another neighbor lived further away, and I wondered what we would do if the first neighbor wasn't home. We could probably make it to the second neighbor's house if we had to, but I didn't know if they would be home either.

Karen didn't have her outside light on, so I could barely see the path leading to her door. Lights in the window filled me with hope and I desperately banged on the door. She opened the door a crack and then gasped when she saw me. "Linda! What's wrong?" I stepped inside to the welcome warmth of her house, and Jake followed. Relief rolled over me with the realization that we would be all right.

I explained my dilemma as Karen filled a tea kettle and set it on the stove to heat. While I waited for the water to boil, my fingers regained their feeling, and I repeatedly thanked her for her help. She loaned me a coat and handed me the tea kettle, then Jake and I plunged back out into the cold.

Arriving at the door, I poured hot water over the key and tried to get it in the door. It went in further than it had earlier, but not all the way. Jake stared at me puzzled that I didn't open the door. Thankfully, I had saved some of the water and poured more of it over the key. This time the key went in and turned. I think Jake was as relieved as I was when the door swung open.

I was tempted to give up and stay home but resolved not to let the little outdoor adventure ruin my evening. I finished getting ready and decided to take a paper cup with milk and honey in it to brew my own coffee at the get-together. I got everything together, threw a coffee pod into my purse and headed toward the door. I had put Karen's coat and tea kettle by the door to drop off on the way to church, so I leaned over to pick those up and proceeded to spill some of the honey and milk out of the cup onto the floor. I couldn't win for losing.

Making Coffee

Arriving at church, I was relieved to just be there, and reasoned that making a cup of coffee would be a simple task. But that was not to be. I discovered that the one-cup coffee maker wasn't in the main kitchen, but was instead in another room not being used that night. When I found the machine, I noticed it wasn't anything like mine at home. I considered how it worked and observed that it didn't hold forty ounces of water like mine did. I filled the reservoir, noting that probably it took about twelve ounces. I figured that since my cup was only ten ounces, the extra water would be there for the next person.

The machine took its own sweet time warming the water. While I waited, I noticed a paper listing requests from the prayer meeting that week, so I picked it up and started reading. After what seemed like a long time, I realized the water pouring into the cup sounded different and looked over to see brown liquid pouring over the top of the cup, rolling over the table and down onto the floor. I grabbed the cup to empty some of it into the trash and burned myself on the hot brew. Apparently, all twelve ounces had emptied out of the machine, and I wouldn't need to worry about the left-over liquid. However, it took quite a while to clean the table and floor of all the excess liquid. I left the room priding myself in how clean the floor and table were, but lamenting that my coffee just didn't taste like I had planned. Later that evening, I drove home praying for a boring weekend. I don't usually have a boring life, but I was certainly wishing for one right then.

I learned a lot from that night. I'm more careful about my storm door, I have a better plan in place to get into my house, and I never take it for granted that I will be able to get back in once I'm out!

"Oh, give thanks to the Lord, for He is good! For His mercy endures forever." Psalm 136:1

I thank God for taking care of Jake and me that night. Things could have gone south quickly, but God protected us, and we are none the worse for our frantic run to Karen's house on that frigid January night.

That whole weekend was another example of God going ahead of me. A heating pipe burst, but a small metal ball kept the water from gushing through my attic. My brother was home and available to help me over the phone. I had plenty of wood and strength to heat the house by other means. I was strong enough to snow blow my own yard, and on Saturday I was able to finish cleaning the rest of the snow off the deck. My neighbor was home that night and happy to help me, and neither I, nor my dog got dangerously cold. I have everything to be thankful for!

"No one ever cared for me like Jesus," C.F. Weigle

CHAPTER TWENTY

HE WAS AHEAD OF ME

"For I, the Lord your God, will hold your right hand,
saying to you, 'Fear not, I will help you.'" Isaiah 41:13

It was a twenty-six-foot travel trailer that had been perfect for our family (the one described in chapter sixteen), but after many years of enjoyment, I decided to sell it. So, I planned to take one last vacation with it and then put it up for sale.

My dad had taught me how to tow the trailer when I bought it six years ago. Thankfully, it was a skill that came back to me even though I only used it once a year. Dad's voice echoed in my head as I watched the lines on the road fade away in the rearview mirrors. "Keep the load in the middle of the road. It takes longer to brake. Never jerk the wheel." These priceless tips and a few others kept me company while I drove the 375 miles to our destination.

My daughter, Sarah, and her husband, Jon, helped me load the camper and we headed out for a relaxing week together. Their car was loaded with tenting supplies and I followed them with the dog as my only companion. My two sons, Mike and Ben, were coming later. I turned up the Southern Gospel Music to drown out the dog's sighs of discontent.

After a week of summer sun, we packed everything back up and I headed toward home – this time without the dog. He rode with my son in his car and I was able to enjoy my music in solitude.

I was halfway home when I felt the trailer rumble as if I had hit a patch of rough pavement. It lasted for about five seconds and then everything calmed down. I decided it must have been an unusual spot on the road. A half-hour later, I stopped for gas and when I was finished pumping, I pulled over to the side of the parking lot.

I got a few snacks out of the trailer and looked at the hitch. There were seven critical spots that must be hooked correctly, and I counted to make sure everything was still secure. Then I walked past the drivers' side of the camper to check the tires, but my heart sank when I saw that the tread on the rear axle tire was peeled down to the steel lining. It looked like the tire had been peeled like an orange. There was no tread to be seen, only bare steel belt. I had never seen anything like it, but I knew I wasn't going anywhere on that tire! I had a spare but knew the whole process of loosening the lug nuts after I got the jack in place was more than I wanted to tackle alone.

"Lord," I prayed. "I need help." I called my daughter to find out where she and her husband were on their journey back to my house, but they were at least a hundred miles ahead of me.

The Phone Book

Taking a deep breath, I walked back across the lot and boldly approached an older gentleman leaning against his car, waiting for the gas pump to shut off. I explained my situation and asked if he could suggest a tow service that would change my tire. He sounded doubtful as he answered, "I don't know. It's a Saturday." Then after a moment, he said, "I have a phone book. We'll look it up." He dug out a well-worn phone book from his car and started looking for numbers.

He suggested a few numbers and after a couple of failed tries, I was able to contact a lady who promised to pass my name and number on to someone else. A minute later my phone rang, and a man said he would be there shortly. I thanked the kind gentleman with the phone book, and he went on his way.

Back at the trailer, I took the spare off the back of the camper and set it beside the bare tire. Then I decided to unhook the hitch so it wouldn't twist when the camper was jacked up on one side. The three points that were the hardest to unhook and re-hook had to be disconnected.

The sun was hot, and my stomach complained loudly about its emptiness. Despite that, I only stopped long enough to sip an iced coffee. I had barely prepared the camper when the mechanic, Greg, arrived in a little VW diesel car. It was an unlikely sight, and I hoped that the man was who he was supposed to be. When he opened the trunk, I was relieved to see a jack with tools to change a tire. Greg was friendly and helpful, even taking my bare tire back to the shop to swap it out for a used one that he said would work in a pinch.

While he was gone, I struggled to get the hitch re-hooked. The camper had moved slightly, even though I had chocked the wheels, and it took a while for me to get everything lined up. The refueling place was busy and several dozen cars came and went while I struggled with the camper, but no one asked if I needed help.

After Greg had delivered my spare, I settled back into the car, relieved to be on my way. I was discouraged about the travel time I had lost, knowing I still had a long way to go. My adult children were staying at my house that night, but would be leaving to finish their trip home the next day, and I didn't want to miss even a moment with them.

I turned up the music and got back on the highway. About eighty miles further down the road I felt a horribly familiar shudder in the trailer and knew I had peeled another tire. Pulling over to the side I got out to see which one had shredded. To my horror it was the spare Greg had just put on the rear axle. Walking around to the other side, my heart sank when I saw that the matching tire on that axle was also bare. Three tires had peeled in less than 100 miles! I was sure that there must be something horribly wrong with the axle that was causing undue stress on the tires. I took a deep breath and forced back the tears stinging my eyes.

A warm summer breeze whistled through the empty fields and rustled the leaves on trees nearby. A few cars flew by, but nobody stopped. I stared in disbelief at the steel belt of the tire, shimmering in the late afternoon sun. Panic threatened to rise in my throat as I considered how desolate my location was. But I shoved it back down, telling myself that God was with me, He had a perfect plan and I was not alone.

A Sign

One lone sign stood by the road declaring that "Ossie's Lunch" was four kilometers down the road. Resolutely, I climbed back into the car, determined to make it to Ossie's. With the emergency flashers warning others that I was only going ten miles an hour, I hugged the shoulder of the road and prayed that the two remaining trailer tires would get me to the exit. I held the steering wheel in such a death grip that several times I had to peel my fingers off one-by-one.

Ossie's was booming with seafood lovers, and I pulled the trailer to the side of the road, being careful not to block the parking lot exit. I was relieved to be there but wondered what to do next. There were no other buildings in sight.

I have roadside assistance on my auto insurance policy, and I prayerfully punched their number into my phone. A nice gentleman on the other end of the phone affirmed that I did have roadside assistance, but that it did not cover the trailer. I pushed the panic back down again, repeating to myself the same sentences I have said to many others. "God is here. He has a plan. This is happening for a reason. I am not alone."

Now that there were people in sight, I didn't know who to trust. "Oh God," I prayed. "I need someone who is capable and honest."

"For He shall give His angels charge over you, to keep you in all your ways." Psalm 91:11

Taking a deep breath, I walked toward a picnic table where two men were waiting for their order. "I'm sorry to bother you, but I need help." After explaining my predicament, one of the men stood up and started walking toward the trailer.

He shook the tires, felt the rims for heat, and crawled under the trailer looking for a problem. "I don't know why your tires peeled, but I don't think your bearings or brakes are the problem." I asked him if there was any way I could get a mechanic to look at my trailer. The man replied, "I am a mechanic. To be truthful, it's desolate here. I don't know of any garages for at least thirty miles. Let's see if we can find a towing company who will do a service call on a Saturday night." He pulled out his phone and started making calls.

People placed orders for their seafood supper at Ossie's counter and order numbers were called out over the loudspeaker. Cars full of hungry families came and left while I stood there holding my phone, wondering what God would do.

By this time, I had called my daughter, Sarah, again, and had also talked with my Dad. I took a deep breath to calm my pounding heart. I was three hours from my nearest family member, and although they were concerned, they couldn't help. They promised to pray, and I knew God was listening.

The Phone Call

The phone rang in my hand and I saw that it was my friend, Al Robbins, calling. God's timing could not have been more perfect. There are two pastoral couples in my life who faithfully call to check on me, and one of them is Al and Laura Robbins. We went to college together, and although we had lost contact with each other, Facebook brought us back together almost a decade ago. They faithfully pray for me every day.

I didn't even say, "Hi." Instead, I answered with, "Al, I need help." I quickly outlined what was happening and he promised to get me help. I had no doubt that he would, because his commanding, yet compassionate personality makes him the type of guy who people respond to.

The mechanic, Trevor, reported that a man was on his way to change the tires. While we were waiting, he crawled under the trailer two more times trying to see what had peeled my tires but could find nothing. A few people came over to stare at my steel tires and to comment in awe. No one had ever seen anything like it.

I kept looking at my phone to see the time, knowing it would be dark soon. Even with new tires I didn't want to try to finish my trip in the dark. It was a three-day holiday for the Canadians, so all the camping areas in the entire region were full. Could I make it over the border and park at a Wal-Mart for the night?

Al called back to tell me he had posted a plea for help on Facebook, saying a widow was in trouble. Several people had responded, and he was working to find out who was the closest to my location. Al and Laura had dropped everything to help me.

The roadside assistance man arrived and jumped out of his truck to look at the tires. "Those tires are old," he announced. "They couldn't take the heat of the load anymore." I thought I had bought new tires for the trailer a while ago, but now I wondered if my memory was as old as the tires.

Trevor stayed and helped me for over half an hour. I remarked that he had to be hungry, but he answered that he had been hungry before, and it was no big deal. His children came over to tell him his food was getting cold, but he didn't leave until the towing company arrived. When he said he was leaving, I shook his hand and thanked him profusely. "God is going to bless you, Trevor, I promise. Watch for it, because He WILL bless you!" Trevor looked doubtful, but politely acknowledged my remarks.

Chris, the roadside assistance man, showed me numbers on the sidewalls of my bare tires. "See this?" he boomed.

"Those numbers say your tires were made in the thirtieth week of 2000. You don't have a problem with your axle, you have a problem with old tires!" He swiftly took the tires off the trailer but struggled to get the old rubber unwound from around the brake drum and leaf springs. He was successful on one side but commented that he would have to bring his crowbar to get the other side cleaned out. Then he left to exchange new tires for the bare ones.

Finally, I listened to my grumbling stomach and ordered a sandwich. Al had called again to say a couple of kind people were on their way to help me. I stood there waiting for my number to be called, wondering what God would do. I was going to be able to move the trailer, but where would I put it? Wal-Mart didn't look like a good prospect any more, since I wouldn't arrive there until after 10 PM.

"God's faithfulness means that God will always do what He said and fulfill what He has promised."
Wayne Grudem

A car pulled in beside my trailer and I could tell the people were looking for someone. Hurrying across the parking lot I recognized Paula, a woman I had gone to college with thirty-five years ago. She had seen the plea for help on Facebook and contacted Al for details. She told me she hadn't been on Facebook all day, but tonight when she turned on the computer, there was Al's message that a widow needed help. She told her husband, Randy, about the post and said, "Ossie's is just a few miles from here!"

Randy and Paula had dropped everything to come help me. We ate together and considered my options for the night. I talked about Wal-Mart, but they mentioned their church would put me up in a motel. That sounded a lot safer to me than Wal-Mart. But when Randy called to see if there was a room available, he was told that all the motels in the area were full because of the holiday.

Chris came back and was able to free the rest of the rubber entwined under the camper by breaking it in pieces with a crowbar and hammer. Then he put the new tires on and assured me once again there was nothing wrong with my axle.

After he left, I asked Randy and Paula if they had an outside water and electric outlet that I could hook my camper to. They assured me that they did and said I was welcome to park in their yard. It was getting dark, I was exhausted, and they only lived a few miles from Ossie's. Gratefully, I followed them to their home, struggling to keep my eyes open during the fifteen-minute ride. I was in no condition to drive forty minutes to the border.

They helped me park and made sure I had everything I needed for the camper. Paula invited me to use their shower, knowing what a long day it had been, then invited me to join them for breakfast the next morning.

After a comforting shower, I collapsed into my cozy bed, overwhelmed by God's goodness at the hand of people I had not seen in thirty-five years. Cloudy skies had threatened rain, but the heavens didn't open until I was warmly tucked into my camper. Listening to the rain pounding on the roof, I considered how different this night could have been. I could have been struggling to get the camper set up alone in a Wal-Mart parking lot during a downpour. Instead warm, caring strangers had kindly seen to my every need.

Once again, God had been ahead of me. He had a man with a phone book pumping gas when I needed a number for roadside assistance. On a desolate stretch of road, I stopped my camper by a sign advertising Ossie's Lunch, a place I had never heard of, and a mechanic was there with his family at the same time I was looking for help. Al Robbins rang my phone while I was standing beside my broken camper. Paula turned on her computer at the same time a plea for help was posted on Facebook. Randy and Paula had only been living in that area for two weeks when they responded to Al's plea.

I drove home the next day without incident, and God was with me every mile of the way. I don't believe in coincidence or luck. Instead, I believe in a God who orders every moment of our lives with perfect purpose. And I'm so glad He does!

CHAPTER TWENTY-ONE

THANKFUL

"Oh, give thanks to The Lord, for He is good; his love endures forever!" Psalm 107:1

"I know of nothing which so stimulates my faith in my Heavenly Father as to look back and reflect on His faithfulness to me in every crisis and every chilling circumstance of life." Philip Keller

Throughout my life, the Lord has been with me. He has loved and provided for me in every circumstance. I am thankful for the care He has given in both good times and bad. It is easy to be thankful when life is going well. But even in times of great trial and turmoil, God has given me so much to be thankful for.

I am thankful for God's unfailing help since the horrible accident that took my husband's life. He has blessed me with lessons learned, prayers answered, and daily Divine guidance.

But I am also thankful for the tears that would not stop, because I can now empathize with a widow's grief as she sobs in my arms. I am thankful for the many months of sleeplessness I endured because I can now recommend sleeping aids and assure her that God is there in the stillness of her night.

I am thankful that I spent unending hours on the phone talking through business decisions with people I did not know about documents I did not understand. There were times I sat at my desk sobbing over obscure paperwork written in various indecipherable wordings. But now I know how to counsel a widow in that regard, and I can advise her who to call to get the answers she needs.

I am thankful that people said stupid, hurtful things, because they had no idea what I was going through. As a result, I can now ask a widow, "Would we really want them to know what we know?" I am thankful that there were no pat answers to soothe my searing soul while watching my children crawl through dark halls of crushing grief. Because now, I have advice to offer young widows about their own broken-hearted children.

I know things that other people do not know. I know that we do not get over grief but instead learn to adjust to it. Although I laugh more and cry less now than I did those years ago, I know that I will always miss Michael, and there will always be unanswered questions. I have turned those questions over to the Lord.

I can tell a widow or a woman in pain that God sees her weeping in the dark and hears the silent groans of her heart. He will give her wisdom when she needs answers, and He is walking ahead of her, getting tomorrow ready for her arrival.

I am thankful that I can offer hope to hurting people during their heartache and horror. I have hugged a grieving grandmother who had recently lost a grandchild. I have never lost a grandchild, but I do understand grief. My credibility comes from having suffered crushing loss. God knew ahead that she would need my comforting words, so He had me in that spot at that time to hold her while she cried.

I have been chosen to walk this path, and I am thankful. Life is short, eternity is forever, and God will make this journey worth it when we reach the other side!

"For I consider that the sufferings of this present time are not worthy to be compared with the glory which shall be revealed in us."
Romans 8:18

NOTES

All Scripture quotes are from NKJV translation unless otherwise noted.

Chapter One – The Accident
Revelation 3:8
Psalm 16:1
Psalm 120:1
Psalm 118:1-2

Chapter Two – I Call Her Mum
Proverbs 31:29
Proverbs 22:6
Moody, D. L. *Moody's Anecdotes and Illustrations: Related in His Revival Work by the Great Evangelist Dwight L. Moody.* Edited by J. B. McClure, Rhodes & McClure, 1899.
Mann, Mirele. "9 George Washington Quotes to Ring in Presidents' Day." *Goodnet: Gateway to Doing Good*, 15 Feb. 2016, www.goodnet.org/articles/9-george-washington-quotes-to-ring-in-presidents-day.

Chapter Three – The Power
Matthew 6:13
Psalm 32:7
Tozer, A. W. *The Knowledge of the Holy.* HarperOne, 1961. Chapter 12, p. 67

Chapter Four – She Was Sick
Psalm 23:4
Psalm 46:1-2
McDaniel, Debbie. *God Will Make a Way Where There Seems to Be No Way*. 22 May 2018,
www.crosswalk.com/devotionals/crosswalk-devo/crosswalk-the-devotional-may-19.html.

Chapter Five– A Very Pregnant Christmas
Jeremiah 29:11
Psalm 139:17-18
"Germany Kent Quotes." *Own Quotes*,
ownquotes.com/profile/germanykent/.

Chapter Six – Stephanie's Prayer
1 Thessalonians 5:7
Jeremiah 29:12
Elliot, Elisabeth. *Let Me Be a Woman*. Tyndale House Publishers, Inc, 2013. p. 9

Chapter Seven– The Decision
Psalm 115:11
Mark 11:24
Isaiah 43:2-3
"Germany Kent Quotes." *Goodreads,*
www.goodreads.com/quotes/8407880-with-god-you-are-stronger-than-your-struggles-and-more.

Chapter Eight– A Closed Window and an Open Door
Proverbs 3:6
Psalm 16:11
Psalm 25:10
Chan, Francis, and Danae Yankoski. *Crazy Love: Overwhelmed by a Relentless God*. David C. Cook, 2013.

Chapter Nine – Heart Attack
Deuteronomy 31:8
James 5:16
Psalm 139:7-10
Pierce, Jerry. "The Father's Hand of Protection." *Decision Magazine*, May 2016, billygraham.org/decision-magazine/may-2016/the-fathers-hand-of-protection/.

Chapter Ten – Perfect Timing
John 3:16
John 14:1-6
Romans 3:23
Romans 6:23
Romans 5:8
Romans 10:9
Romans 10:13
Romans 5:1
Romans 8:1
Romans 8:38-39
Piper, John. *Desiring God: Meditations of a Christian Hedonist*. Multnomah Books, 2017.

Chapter Eleven – Forget Me Not
Matthew 28:20
Malachi 3:6
"Elisabeth Elliot Quotes." *Women of Christianity*,
womenofchristianity.com/quotes/elisabeth-elliot-
quotes/.

Chapter Twelve – The Prayer Shawl
Luke 22:32
John 17:9-10
Fenelon, Francois. *AZQuotes.com*, Wind and Fly, LTD,
2019, www.azquotes.com/author/4732-
Francois_Fenelon.

Chapter Thirteen – Our Anniversary
1 Thessalonians 5:24
Hebrews 10:23
Spurgeon, Charles. *Morning & Evening*. Discovery House,
2016. p.142

Chapter Fourteen – His Birthday
Hebrews 13:5
Psalm 34:18
Grosse, Alexander. *The Happiness of Enjoying, and
Making a True and Speedy Use of Christ: Setting Forth,
First, the Fulness of Christ : Secondly, the Danger of
Neglecting Christ ... : Thirdly, the Lord Jesus the Soules
Last Refuge ... : Whereunto Is Added, S. Pauls Legacie, or
Farewell to the Men of Corinth [rule]*. London: Printed by
Tho. Brudenell, for John Bartlet, 1647. Print.

Chapter Fifteen - The Car
Lamentations 3:7
Psalm 32:8
Stanley, Charles F. *Life Principle 14: God Acts on Our Behalf*. 14 July, 2014,
https://www.intouch.org/read/life-principle-14-god-acts-on-our-behalf

Chapter Sixteen – Wait
Psalm 27:14
Psalm 25:5
"Jim Elliot Quotes." *BrainyQuote*, 2019,
www.brainyquote.com/citation/quotes/jim_elliot_189251

Chapter Seventeen – Coffee
Psalm 139:3
Isaiah 30:21
1 Thessalonians 4:9
Crouse, Carl. "You May Be the Only Bible Some People Read, 1 Tim. 4.11-5.2." *Sumas A.C. Church*, 4 Jan. 2011,
www.sumasacchurch.com/sermons/you-may-be-the-only-bible-some-people-read-1-tim-411-52.

Chapter Eighteen – Leaky Pipes and Frozen Doors: Part One
Psalm 59:16
Psalm 91:2
Pink, A. W. "The Faithfulness of God." *The Reformed Reader*, 1999, www.reformedreader.org/aog02.htm.

Chapter Nineteen – Leaky Pipes and Frozen Doors: Part Two
Isaiah 43:2
Psalm 136:1
Weigle, C. F. "No One Ever Cared for Me like Jesus."
Copyright ©1932 by Singspiration Music

Chapter Twenty – He Was Ahead of Me
Isaiah 41:13
Psalm 91:11
Grudem, Wayne. *Systematic Theology: An Introduction to Biblical Doctrine.* Harper Collins, 2009. p.177

Chapter Twenty-One – Thankful
Psalm 107:1
Romans 8:18
Keller, W. Phillip. *A Shepherd Looks at Psalm 23.* Zondervan, 2015.